Critical Essays on Major Curriculum Theorists

D0076243

Critical Essays on Major Curriculum Theorists is a critical appreciation of the work of ten leading curriculum theorists from the fields of education, philosophy, sociology and psychology. For thirty years in the UK and round the world, the curriculum has been the subject of an intense debate about its content and form.

The substantive argument of this book is the need for a new model of curriculum, one which supports a conception of education as the public good. It therefore revisits some of the major curriculum issues that have surfaced over the last thirty years with the intention of providing alternatives to the official way that curriculum is now understood.

This invaluable critical commentary is intended for the research community and for students looking for an introduction to some of the key educational thinkers of our time. The book:

- offers a broad range of international perspectives on the curriculum;
- contributes to a deeper understanding of the curriculum;
- presents alternative models of curriculum;
- examines the rationale for education as a public good;
- develops the field of curriculum whilst bringing together important existing work.

David Scott is Professor of Educational Leadership and Learning at the University of Lincoln, UK.

Critical Essays on Major Curriculum Theorists

David Scott

Routledge
Taylor & Francis Group

LONDON AND NEW YORK

First published 2008
by Routledge
2 Park Square, Milton Park, Abingdon, Oxon OX14 4RN

Simultaneously published in the USA and Canada
by Routledge
270 Madison Ave, New York, NY 10016

Routledge is an imprint of the Taylor & Francis Group, an informa business

Typeset in Garamond by
Keystroke, 28 High Street, Tettenhall, Wolverhampton
Printed and bound in Great Britain by
TJ International Ltd, Padsow, Cornwall

British Library Cataloguing in Publication Data
A catalogue record for this book is available from the British Library

Library of Congress Cataloging in Publication Data
Scott, David, 1951–
    Critical essays on major curriculum theorists / David Scott.
        p. cm.
    Includes bibliographical references and index.
    1. Education–Curricula–Philosophy. 2. Curriculum change–Philosophy. I. Title.
    LB1570.S356 2007
    375'.0001—dc22
    2007004673

ISBN10: 0–415–33984–7 (hbk)
ISBN10: 0–415–33983–9 (pbk)
ISBN10: 0–203–46188–6 (ebk)

ISBN13: 978–0–415–33984–1 (hbk)
ISBN13: 978–0–415–33983–4 (pbk)
ISBN13: 978–0–203–46188–4 (ebk)

To Moira, Sarah and Ben, with thanks and love

Contents

Tables

Acknowledgements

Parts of Chapters 5, 9 and 11 originally appeared in Scott (2000; 2003; 2005) and Scott *et al.* (2004). Each of these extracts has been extensively revised. Permission to use this material has been given by The Open University Press, Sage Publications and RoutledgeFalmer.

Chapter I

Introduction

Jerome Bruner (1996, p. 62) makes the point that 'there is something special about "talking" to authors, now dead but alive in their ancient texts – so long as the objective of the encounter is not worship but discourse and "going meta" on thoughts about the past.' This book is an engagement with the past, though many of the curriculum theorists referred to here are still very much alive. It is an engagement with the past that takes seriously Bruner's suggestion that discourse, critique and even 'going meta' are worthwhile. The sense of critique which pervades this book is not intended as a negative rebuttal of the theories and ideas developed by the various curriculum theorists referred to in the chapters that follow, but a building on and reinvigorating of their work. Each of them focuses on an idea central to an understanding of the curriculum; so, for example, W. J. Popham (1972) advocates a behavioural objectives view of the curriculum, whereas Lawrence Stenhouse (1967; 1975) argues for a process form of curriculum. Other curriculum theorists, though their work is much wider than is suggested here, offer perspectives on foundationalism (Paul Hirst, 1974a; 1974b; 1993); power-knowledge (Michel Foucault, 1977; 1984); social structures (Michael Apple, 1979; 1982; 1988; 1996, 2000); pedagogy (Basil Bernstein, 1975; 1985; 1990; 1996); internalisation (Lev Vygotsky, 1978; 1991; 1999); psycho-cultural views of learning (Jerome Bruner, 1960; 1966; 1971; 1983; 1996); critical pedagogy (Henri Giroux, 1981; 1983; 1988; 1989; 1992; 1994); reflection (Donald Schon, 1983; 1987); and autonomy (John White, 1973; 1982; 1990; 1997).

First, a brief look at writing history. A history of the curriculum and of curriculum ideas rarely finds general agreement amongst practitioners as to what it should be. Whether we adopt a conventional view of history with its transhistorical subject or we seek to genealogise history by subverting the 'naturalness' of the categories and delineations used in commonsense discourses, we still have to confront our own position as historian or genealogist. That is, we still have to come to terms with the originary status of our own viewpoint about knowledge.

Any study of curriculum ideas therefore constitutes knowledge about knowledge, and this adds to its complexity. Further to this, knowledge is formed, disseminated and reconstituted in specific historical circumstances, and frequently as a response to them. Usher (1997) suggests in relation to finding out about the world that knowledge has a con-text, pre-text, sub-text and inter-text; and this applies to historical knowledge as much as it does to learning in the curriculum. Historical research for him is a textual practice. The context comprises the situatedness of the historian in the act of writing history so that they are immersed in structures or significations of gender, sexuality, ethnicity or class. Furthermore, the historian is situated within various pre-texts or discourses about the way the world is structured so that their writing is always underpinned by pre-organised meanings. The pre-text in turn has attached to it a sub-text, in that the writing strategy and the knowledge which is subsumed within it are distinctive ways of knowing the world. Finally, any account makes reference to other knowledge constructs and other historical meaning formations – the inter-text. Con-texts, pre-texts, sub-texts and inter-texts are interlaced with notions of power and control, which are foregrounded in any history of the curriculum.

For Michel Foucault (see Chapter 5 below), power and domination have conventionally been understood in terms of something being done by someone to another, and in the process dominating, restricting, coercing this other. These forms of power have been criticised by Foucault for being excessively negative in orientation, and for ignoring the productive forms of power that allow us to go on in life. In other words, power is ever present and never more so than in the knowledge mechanisms, discourses and inscribed subjectivities that make up reality. The role of the genealogist is to uncover or decipher the rules that constitute particular formations of power, whether of a coercive or productive kind, and to do so without becoming embroiled in logo-centric discourses.

To do otherwise is to fall into the trap of what Foucault (1977) calls the illusion of formalisation, in which the historian attempts to explain types of knowledge in terms of a formal logic that transcends those knowledge constructions: a logo-centric viewpoint. Foucault also enjoins us to avoid the illusion of doxa where appearances in relation to power are treated as opportunities to unmask them and replace them with more truthful versions of events and activities.

This would suggest that we cannot step outside those subjectivities, forms of ascribed behaviours and discourses that constitute our lives and the life of our society, even as historians. This means that we abandon notions of illogicality, false thinking, deception, and operate through a pure form of discourse. All we have is the discourse or at least a number of discourses, each of which has its own form of logic, its own particular relation to practices and behaviours, its own form of relations between items, its own way of determining which items of knowledge are valid and which are not and its own way of ascribing evaluative content to those items and combinations of those items. Furthermore, analysis of these discursive regimes always originates from another discursive regime. The theorist therefore operates outside other discursive regimes, looking in, as it were, from a position which never quite captures them in their entirety.

Though we do not have wholly to accept such a view of the historian-at-work, this does point to a number of problems that any historian of ideas has to confront. First, there is a danger of treating any body of ideas as separate from the historical, socio-political and geographical circumstances from which it emerged. Second, there is a tendency for this body of ideas to be judged by criteria developed in a later period of time or in terms of a universal or trans-cendental set of criteria – Foucault's (1977) illusion of formalisation. Third, there is a danger that any interpretation or retelling of ideas developed by someone else and in a different time period is taken to constitute a definitive reading of that work. As the curriculum is a selection from all the available knowledge which has been developed, so are readings from key writers about that curriculum. There is a further danger if the whole corpus of writings of a single individual is treated as coherent and consistent. Writers change their minds; they develop their ideas; they even in certain cases reject the essential elements of their previous work. Ludwig Wittgenstein, for example, in his second major work, the *Philosophical Investigations* (1953), developed a prag-matic and socio-cultural view of language which is essentially at odds with the correspondence view of reality that he argued for in his earlier work, the *Tractatus Logico-Philosophicus* (1961). For these reasons, the historian of ideas has to tread carefully, and even more so if his or her subject matter is the curriculum, since decisions about what should be included and what should be excluded from it are deeply embedded in socio-political processes.

At times in what follows, I will be arguing against the positions taken up by these curriculum theorists; in other words, I will be pointing to incon-sistencies, irregularities, contradictions, muddles and aporias where I find them. At other points in the text, I will be attempting to present their ideas as models of curriculum which were influential in their particular *époque*. Elsewhere, I will be taking out of context a particular set of ideas they developed in order to work on it, re-contextualise it, and in the process present it anew. The result will be an unconventional history, but nevertheless a history which I hope pays due deference to the intellectual work of some influential curriculum theorists.

Two models of curriculum

How therefore can we characterise current formations of curriculum? Basil Bernstein (1996) identified two models of curriculum and called these *performance* and *competence*, with the former now the dominant model round the world. From his earliest work on language, classification and framing to his later work on specialised semiotic codes, Bernstein has had a profound effect on curriculum theory (see Chapter 7 below). Highly abstract in formulation, he offers schemata that open up the possibility of understanding practices of cultural transmission and social reproduction. His two models give different emphases or weightings to the various curriculum dimensions, and are therefore 'distinguished by time, space and discourse (whether content was presented as subjects or themes), evaluation, control, pedagogic text (whether the learner's output or what the teacher sees it as signifying), autonomy and economy' (Fitz *et al.*, 2006, p. 6).

The performance model has its origins in the behavioural objectives movement, and though contested by curriculum theorists, retains its status as the dominant model. It is a model which clearly emphasises marked subject boundaries, traditional forms of knowledge, explicit realisation and recognition rules for pedagogic practice, and the designation and establishment of strong boundaries between different types of students. Fitz *et al.* (2006, p. 6) describe this model in the following way:

> Space and movement were likely to be strongly marked. With the focus upon acquirers' past and future accomplishments, with strong, apparent progression and pacing, evaluation focused on what was missing from the texts in terms of explicit and specific criteria of which they were made aware. Their texts were products of their performance, to be graded and repair systems made available to those who did not meet them. Order was strongly relayed through explicit positional control.

Such a model in the hands of policy-makers becomes both normative and teleological. Furthermore, in policy texts, it has been combined – in the sense that elements of it can act as proxies for liberal and progressive ideologies – with discourses that seem to reflect a politics that offers a break with the past. Thus, *repair* is a tokenistic word to indicate that what was once broken can be put right; *explicit criteria* offer a vision of the future which suggests that muddle can be circumvented.

Bernstein compares this with a competence model, and in relation to the latter, he suggests that acquirers have some control over the selection, pacing and sequencing of their curriculum. For Bernstein, performance modes were seen as the norm, whereas competence modes 'may be seen as interrupts or resistances to this normality or may be appropriated by official education for specific and local purposes', and 'were generally found regulating the early life of acquirers or in repair sections' (Bernstein, 1996, p. 65). However, performance modes are being increasingly applied to early years' education and children with special needs, since recent developments in the UK, for example, have shown that policy-makers are prepared to move from a competence to a performance mode here as well. It is of course clear that underpinning discourses only become dominant through specific sets of historical circumstances, including technological developments, and particular sets of policy enactments; and further to this, that within the policy cycle, there is space for resistance to particular modes of thought and imposed practices.

Governments round the world therefore at the end of the twentieth century and in the early part of the twenty-first century, with a few notable exceptions, have reached a settlement about the nature of the school curriculum. This has meant that key ideas and themes which surfaced at particular moments in the history of the curriculum have been put to one side, and a false consensus on curriculum, barely agreed and certainly not negotiated, has replaced what was once a vigorous debate about central educational questions and in particular questions that related to the curriculum. This consensus now operates at all levels of the education system, and can be expressed in terms of a number of propositions: traditional knowledge forms and strong insulations between them need to be preserved; each of these knowledge forms can be expressed in terms of lower- and higher-level domains and the latter have to be taught before the former and sequenced correctly; certain groups of children are better able to access the curriculum than other children, and thus a differentiated curriculum is necessary to meet the needs of all school learners; the teacher's role is to impart this body of knowledge in the most efficient and effective way, and thus their brief can concern itself not with the ends to which education is directed, but only with the means for its efficient delivery; and the school's role is to deliver a public service that meets the targets set for it by governments. As Bernstein (1990, p. 25) suggests, strong boundaries and clear insulations can be said to characterise this consensus:

> Punctuations are written by power relations that establish as the order of things distinct subjects through distinct voices. Indeed, insulation is the means whereby the cultural is transformed into the natural, the contingent into the necessary, the past into the present, the present into the future.

Webster's *Revised Unabridged Dictionary* (1913) gives two meanings to the word *etiolated*. The first is 'to become white or whiter; to be whitened or blanched by excluding the light of the sun, as plants'; and the second is 'to become pale through disease or absence of light'. We have perhaps now an etiolated curriculum debate, with Bernstein's performance mode in the ascendancy.

Curriculum episodes

A history of the curriculum can be treated as a series of episodes. Each of these episodes overlaps, persists, reconstitutes itself in a different guise and inserts itself into practice in a different way. It is possible to identify seven episodes: scientific curriculum-making; intrinsic worthwhile knowledge; innovative pedagogical experimentation; socio-cultural learning; critical pedagogy; instrumentalism; and school effectiveness/school improvement, though labelling them as such may serve to construct artificial chronological and historical boundaries round them. The story begins with the construction of scientific curriculum-making, where the process of teaching and learning is subsumed into a narrative about the correct way of developing curricula. Alongside it and indeed preceding it is a foundationalist view of knowledge which emphasises its intrinsic worthwhileness. Opposed to this view, and setting itself up as an oppositional discourse to scientific curriculum-making, is the notion of teaching and learning as an innovative pedagogical experiment. Interwoven between them are various forms of instrumentalism. These four episodes are essentially focused on the construction of the curriculum; however, curriculum theorists sought to develop theories about how people learn, and thus foreground the notion of pedagogy and, in Jerome Bruner's case, socio-cultural learning. This position in time gave way to the advocacy of a form of critical pedagogy, and from there to the development of a post-modern curriculum. All this time, scientific curriculum theorists, now in the guise of school effectiveness/school improvement theorists, were working to reassert the primacy of curriculum as a scientific discipline.

Scientific curriculum-making

Kliebard (1975) reminds us of the genesis of the curriculum movement in the United States, and identifies two key figures in the early part of the last century who represent this surge of enthusiasm for the application of the scientific method to the study and implementation of the curriculum. Franklin Bobbitt and Werrett Charters in their different ways argued for precision, objectivity, prediction and the use of the scientific method to establish once and for all what should be taught in schools and indeed how educational knowledge should be structured. Bobbitt's two major works were, appropriately enough, *The Curriculum* (1918) and *How to Make a Curriculum* (1924), and in 1913 he published a long article entitled, 'Some General Principles of Management Applied to the Problems of City-school Systems'. Charters' two major works were *Methods of Teaching: Developed from a Functional Standpoint* (1909) and *Curriculum Construction* (1923), both of which reflected then currently fashionable ideas of structural-functionalism.

Bobbitt's work provides an early example of the arguments for behavioural objectives and he is credited with developing a notion of objective analysis whereby designated skills are broken down into their constituent elements. These skills were derived from the activities of experts in a variety of fields essential to the well-being of society, and he claimed that curricular aims could be derived from an objective examination of these activities. Furthermore, these skills and their component sub-skills could be expressed as specific teaching objectives which could be so arranged that the curriculum could be designed around them. His work was behaviourist in that he understood learning as the acquiring of these skills and the evaluation of sets of behaviours so as to determine whether those skills had been successfully acquired by the learner. It is easy to see here the origin of the behavioural objectives movement which influenced curriculum-making in the 1970s and 1980s and which continues to shape national and local curricula round the world.

What is noteworthy is the underpinning belief in science as the model for the essential practical activity of determining what should be included in a curriculum and how it should be delivered. Thus atomism, pre-specification and control are foregrounded, with the curriculum conceptualised in terms of behavioural objectives and an input-output model of schooling. Ralph Tyler (1950; 1968), for example, advocated a means-end approach to the development of the curriculum. He believed that educational aims could only be articulated in terms of objectives and that these preceded learning experiences and the evaluation of what is learnt. Curriculum-making was understood as a linear process which starts with the development of clear objectives or goals, proceeds to the selection of content which is specified in behavioural terms – that is, its acquisition must be an observable or testable process – and finishes with the evaluation of that process to see if those objectives have been met. However, he did not believe that objectives could be specified in precise behavioural terms, and he believed that they should be kept at a fairly general level. His work has influenced current models of policy-making and curriculum, though his objectives approach has in turn been heavily criticised for its limited understanding of the enacted curriculum. Other theorists such as W. J. Popham (1972; see also Chapter 2 below) were less discriminating about the use of behavioural objectives and were enthusiastic advocates of a scientific view of curriculum-making. Such a position was underpinned by a view of knowledge which coloured their perception of the curriculum. In the USA and the UK a behavioural objectives model formed the centre-piece for recently introduced national curricula.

This behavioural objectives model has been criticised (cf. Elliott, 1998) for the following reasons: complex and important learning outcomes of any educational programme may be neglected at the expense of the more trivial and less important, because it is easier to describe the latter in behavioural objective terms. The pre-specification of behavioural goals may also encourage an inflexibility of approach within the classroom, and learning outcomes which may incidentally flow from classroom interactions will be deliberately under-exploited. There is a further danger of assuming that if something cannot be measured, then it cannot be assessed and therefore it should not be a part of the learning process. Finally, lists of intended behaviours do not adequately represent the way individuals learn, and this is because logical order cannot be conflated with pedagogic process.

In opposition to behavioural objectives, it has been suggested that curriculum theorists should designate appropriate processes which learners need to go through. This avoids the problems inherent in the designation of pre-specified behavioural objectives noted above and builds into the curriculum a more active and influential role for the teacher. Lawrence Stenhouse (1967; 1975; see also Chapter 3) was a trenchant critic of the use of behavioural objectives. Though his published writings are sparse due to his premature death, his work on the curriculum is still influential. It focused on the teacher-as-researcher, the limitations of a behavioural objectives curriculum model and the centrality of the teacher to the enacted curriculum.

Intrinsically worthwhile knowledge

In the 1970s and 1980s curriculum theorists were concerned with knowledge, and in particular transcendental knowledge, which provided a rationale or justification for the school curriculum. Shorn of its metaphysical under-pinnings, such an argument can be expressed in a number of ways. White (1982, p. 10) suggests one such interpretation:

> The argument is at its most plausible when used to justify the particular claim that the pursuit of *knowledge* is intrinsically worthwhile. It asserts that if anyone either doubts or denies the claim, he [*sic*] can be brought to see, assuming he is a rational person, that there is an ineradicable incon-sistency in his position. For in asking 'why pursue knowledge?', the sceptic is in fact already committed to the pursuit of what he is attempt-ing to justify: it is presupposed to his seriously asking the question that he thinks it worthwhile to try to arrive at a well-grounded true belief about the topic in question, i.e. to come to know something.

As White goes on to suggest, this argument is flawed in so far as asking the particular question about the pursuit of knowledge in a general sense does not commit one to the pursuit of all types of knowledge per se; and furthermore, it does not provide any justification for deciding that some types of knowledge are more worthwhile than other types of knowledge. Thus, even if the first part of the argument is accepted, there are no grounds within the argument presented here for determining what that knowledge should be.

A view of knowledge as intrinsically worthwhile has persisted for a long time; for example, Aristotle (1925) presents his readers with the following argument. The purpose of life is predetermined, as is the individual's nature, though it is not always clear to the individual themselves what this natural purpose is. However, a lack of clarity can be remedied through rational delib-eration and reflection on the self; and it is the possession of reason which distinguishes human beings from other animals. If this is accepted, then the end-point of human life is to pursue this aim; and thus from this set of premises can be deduced the aim of education as the pursuit of rational activities that develop the mind. It is fairly easy to see how this syllogism rests on false or at least disputed premises, so that predetermination and a fixed nature are concepts that are not readily accepted in the modern era.

However, what has persisted is a foundationalist view of epistemology; Paul Hirst's work exemplifies this (see Chapter 4 below). His early work identified forms of knowledge through reason which structure the curriculum. His later work moved beyond this and attempted a reformulation of these ideas with the curriculum understood as initiation into social practices. This in turn is understood as knowledge, attitudes, feelings, virtues, skills, dispositions and relationships. However, recent developments in the field of epistemology now offer a serious critique of a foundationalist view of knowledge.

It has already been suggested that a curriculum is always a selection from a range of human activities. Foundationalist justifications for inclusion in a curriculum offer reasons for including some forms of activities and excluding others, and there are perhaps three types. These are: logical delineations between domains of knowledge, distinctive mental or cognitive operations, and cross-cultural social distinctions. An example of logical delineations is Hirst's (1974b) forms of knowledge and experience: logico-mathematical, empirical, interpersonal, moral, aesthetic, religious and philosophical. Each of these forms has distinctive kinds of concepts, and distinctive ways of determining truth from falsehood. Hirst claimed therefore that each has a separate logical form. An example of the second type of justification is Gardner's (1983) seven forms of intelligence: language or linguistic intelligence, logical-mathematical analysis, spatial representation, musical analysis, bodily kinaesthetic thinking, interpersonal knowledge and intrapersonal knowledge. His justification for inclusion of these forms of intelligence is psychological: individual learners have cognitive or mental modules which are separate and act separately from other mental modules. Individuals have been shown to differ in their capacity to perform these different types of operations. A third set of justifications moves us out of the mind and focuses on the culture we inhabit. Lawton (1989) argues that all societies have cultural sub-systems: socio-political, economic, communicative, rational, technological, moral, belief-related, aesthetic and maturational. Because these are universal and cross-cultural, Lawton concludes that curriculum developers should seek to represent the forms of knowledge which underpin them.

Progression within a curriculum can also take a foundationalist form. Underpinning the notion of progression is a rationale for teaching some aspects of the knowledge domain before others and a belief that a subject can in fact be arranged in a reliable hierarchy. Adey (1997) argues that it is possible to do this and develops a three-dimensional model comprising conceptual complexity, breadth and extent. Using only the last of these two dimensions leads to a naive view of learning. For Adey, a measure of conceptual complexity is also needed to provide a fully developed model of curriculum progression. Examples of these frameworks are: Piaget's (1971) schema comprising progression from concrete operational to formal operational thinking, and Kohlberg's (1976) stages of moral thought, where the subject progresses from pre-moral and conventional rule conformity levels to the acceptance of general rights and standards, and even to adopting individual principles of conduct. These hierarchies are based on empirical investigation. The other way of establishing knowledge hierarchies is through some form of logical ordering, where complexity comprises both a progressive development of more items of knowledge and the making of more complicated connections between these items of knowledge. Such foundationalist views are in conflict with instrumentalist views discussed elsewhere in this book.

Innovative pedagogical experiment

A third episode in the history of curriculum ideas designates the curriculum as an innovative pedagogical experiment. Elliott (1998) sets out the key themes and ideas that constitute this form of curriculum-making. He describes social change as continuous, and difficult to predict scientifically and control socially. Furthermore, it is dynamic and complex, rather than episodic, stable, static and involving simple entities. Furthermore, modern societies are risk societies with fluid boundaries and shifting identities. Responsibility for shaping lives cannot therefore be left to governments alone, but should be devolved to individuals themselves. Here, Elliott is suggesting a form of grassroots democracy, in which schools and education services have an important part to play. The traditional curriculum is ill served to meet the demands placed on people in different and changing circumstances, and for Elliott, the task is to appropriate cultural resources to enable individuals to take responsibility for their lives. Furthermore, the traditional, strongly classified and strongly framed curriculum configures those cultural resources in a way that is accessible to only a few and not to the many. A curriculum which is responsive to the needs of all pupils has to take a particular form:

> More consistent with such an aim is a curriculum which organises cultural resources in usable forms for the purposes of enabling pupils to deepen and extend their understanding of the problems and dilemmas of everyday life in society, and to make informed and intelligent judgements about how they might be resolved. Such a curriculum will be responsive to pupils' own thinking and their emerging understandings and insights into human situations. It will therefore be continuously tested, reconstructed and developed by teachers as part of the pedagogical process itself, rather than in advance of it. Hence, the idea of 'pedagogically driven' curriculum change as an innovative experiment.
>
> (Elliott, 1998, p. xiii)

Elliott distinguishes between curriculum and pedagogy, but suggests that there should be a focus on both, and on teachers as curriculum experimenters and action researchers. Furthermore, the action researcher element should be treated not as another strategy for the better delivery of educational ends developed elsewhere but as an essential part of the development of the curriculum per se. Educational change, for Elliott, involves reflection by teachers on the 'problematics of their curriculum and pedagogic practices' (1998, p. xiii). The implications of understanding the curriculum as an innovative pedagogical experiment and teachers as innovators presupposes a view of society as a community of educated people which is in opposition to technicist and market-orientated approaches. Planning by objectives 'distorts the nature of knowledge and leaves little room for individuals to use our culture as a medium for the development of their own thinking in relation to the things that matter in life' (Elliott, 1998, p. xiv).

Socio-cultural models of learning

A further episode in the history of the curriculum focuses on pedagogy and the development of socio-cultural models of learning. For example, Jerome Bruner's (1960; 1966; see also Chapter 9 below) early work represents an exploration of intrapsychic processes of knowing and learning, and the development of ideas such as the spiral curriculum and the three modes of understanding: enactive, iconic and symbolic. His later work represents a reformulation of psychology from its behaviourist form, and a development of cultural psychology, so that meaning, narrative and intrapersonal communication become increasingly important concerns. Bruner's work on curriculum echoes and pays due deference to the earlier work of Lev Vygotsky (1978; see also Chapter 8 below), and Vygotsky's influence on the field of curriculum and more generally on the field of education has been profound. He described his theory as cultural-historical, and he meant by this that mind, cognition and memory can only be understood as functions that are carried out with other people and in society. He developed two important notions: *the zone of proximal development* and *inner speech*, both of which have contributed since the mid-1970s to a revolution in pedagogy. However, as will become apparent, policy developments round the world, and in particular in the USA and the UK, have combined to restrict the impact of these new pedagogic forms. Bruner's much quoted and controversial maxim, for example, that 'any subject can be taught effectively in some intellectually honest form to any child at any stage of development' (1960, p. 33) reflects a view of pedagogy and curriculum which is at variance with the development of strong boundaries between forms of knowledge and between types of children encapsulated in Bernstein's performance model of curriculum.

Bruner and Vygotsky, though with different emphases, foreground society and culture as key dimensions of learning, and this is in contrast to imitative and didactic forms of pedagogy. A number of different models of pedagogy, then, have been developed. The first of these is imitation. Learners seek to copy the actions of the teacher and in the process incorporate these observed characteristics into their behaviours. Much learning of an informal nature, especially in early childhood, takes this form. Didacticism, on the other hand, involves instruction where the teacher inculcates a knowledge, skill or affective domain into learners by informing them about what they should do and how they should behave. This view of pedagogy has been disputed by constructivists and situationists who understand learning as contextualised, and thus as incapable of being understood without reference to the environment in which it takes place. Constructivists and situationists have developed a notion of inter-subjective interchange in which learners construct knowledge in the light of the experiences they have in and outwith the classroom, and in the process create meanings for themselves and others. The fourth pedagogic approach is apprenticeship in which the learner is supported in their attempts to gain access to the culture of the society in which they are being educated.

The two most important learning theories, symbol-processing and situated cognitive approaches, allocate distinctive roles to learning styles, assessment and meta-cognition. Symbol-processing approaches understand the learner and the environment as separate; learning takes place within the human mind as the individual processes information they receive through their senses, assimilates that information and creates new ways of understanding. This theory positions the individual as a passive recipient of environmental influences. It separates out mind from body, language from reality and the individual from society. Situated cognition understands the relationship between the individual and the environment in a different way. Situated learning approaches view the person and the environment as mutually constructed and mutually constructing. Bredo (1999) suggests that this relationship should be viewed actively and as involving dynamic modification rather than static matching. The learner acts with and on the environment, shaping or modifying themselves and at the same time shaping or modifying the environment. Situated cognitive approaches stress active, transformative and relational dimensions to learning; indeed, situated cognitionists understand learning as contextualised.

This has led in turn, principally through Donald Schon's (1983) critique of technical rationality, to an emphasis on reflection and meta-reflection within the context of learning communities, with society once again foregrounded, in contrast to theories of learning which understand the learner as a passive imbiber of information from their environment. Schon's (see Chapter 11 below) best work can be found in his two seminal books, *The Reflective Practitioner* (1983) and *Educating the Reflective Practitioner* (1987). In particular, his attack on various forms of technical rationality has been a major influence on post-compulsory education discourses. Reflection and reflective practices have become central ideas for the construction of professional development courses in a range of disciplines. Schon's (1987) well-known distinction between reflection-in-action and reflection on reflection-in-action is the central theme of new developments in learning and pedagogy in this field.

Much of the work on professional development since the mid-1980s has focused on teaching and learning, with a subsequent neglect of both assessment practices and the impact assessment has on both formal learning settings and the workplace. Teaching and learning strategies on professional development courses have utilised a range of methods. The first of these is instruction, whether hierarchical or progressive (Adey, 1997), spiral (Bruner, 1996), sequenced (Gagne, 1985), or modular. The second is coaching in situ, understood as the learner being offered feedback and critique as they perform the skills required in the workplace. Collins *et al.* (1989) have developed a coaching model for professional development that includes: modelling by the expert; coaching while the learner practises; scaffolding where the learner is supported during the initial stages with that support gradually being withdrawn as the learner becomes more proficient; articulation during the learning process; reflection on those processes and comparison with the expert's reasons for action; and exploration where the learner undertakes various workplace activities without support. Third, there is observation where the learner either mimics the expert performing in the desired role or identifies with and emulates that person (Bandura, 1986). Associated with this is the notion of role modelling, where the learner identifies with the role model: partially, charismatically, performatively, optionally or negatively (Bucher and Stelling, 1977). Fourth, there is the process of mentoring, whether built into professional development courses or developed informally. Fifth, there are processes of simulation and transfer. Simulation provides a proxy experience for the learner outside the workplace, and the intention is that those skills can then be transferred to real-life situations. Generic theories of transfer suggest that the professional can develop certain general skills and attributes which then enable improvements to their performance in non-related areas. Identical elements theory suggests that transfer only occurs when enough of the elements are shared between the learning site and the workplace setting.

Within this framework of situated learning, a new model of apprenticeship has been developed. The traditional model is characterised as a conservative and static transmission framework: only the apprentice learns; the body of knowledge being transmitted is fixed and unproblematic; the expert teaches and does not learn from the experience; and the knowledge that is acquired is context-bound and not transferable. Guile and Young (1999) contrast this with a form of apprenticeship that understands learning as an active, social and collective process that takes place in a community of practice. Contexts within which that learning takes place are always changing; and more importantly, new knowledge emerges for both the expert and the apprentice.

Practitioner learning in the light of these new developments is therefore understood as contextualised and situation-specific. Universities, however, are offering courses on professional development to in-service educational practitioners which are taught away from the practice site, frequently operate within technicist frameworks of understanding, and adopt disciplinary forms of knowledge. That is, knowledge developed outside the practice setting is made available to students who are then required to apply it to their own practice. This knowledge may take the form of models of good practice or ideal simulations of what the practitioner should be doing in the practice setting. The knowledge being developed is generalisable, and moves beyond the repertoire of actions with which the practitioner is familiar. This can be contrasted with informal, work-specific and transitory forms of knowledge. For Schon, knowledge underpinned by a technical rationality model fails to take account of the context-specific nature of knowledge acquisition. Schon himself has been criticised, in turn, for not developing a critical approach to knowledge.

Critical pedagogy

Critical pedagogy is underpinned by a belief that schooling and the curriculum 'always represent[s] an introduction to, preparation for, and legitimation of particular forms of life' (McLaren, 1989, p. 160). It thus seeks, through pedagogic means, to surface and in the process disrupt conventional forms of understanding which serve to reproduce undemocratic, racist, sexist and unequal social relations. As Lankshear et al. (1996, p. 150) make clear,

> [t]he task of critical pedagogy . . . is to unmask hegemonies and critique ideologies with the political and ethical intent of helping to empower students and more generally, the social groups to which they belong: by fostering awareness of conditions that limit possibilities for human becoming and legitimate the unequal distribution of social goods.

Unlike some post-modern viewpoints, critical pedagogy is predicated on a clear ethical position with regard to society and to the way society reproduces itself, though some versions of critical pedagogy emphasise the need to disrupt conventional school knowledge structures and the reproductive processes that accompany them without specifying alternative frames of reference for students. The end-point becomes the disruptive process rather than the re-forming of schooling and society in a particular way.

Lankshear et al. (1996) suggest that critical pedagogy had to wrestle with a number of serious problems. Though implicit within it is a notion of student-centredness and student empowerment, all too frequently teachers found it difficult to forgo their role as orchestrators of proceedings, thus in effect critical pedagogy became a means by which one ideological viewpoint replaced another. Structural constraints on the implementation of critical pedagogic processes proved to be difficult to negotiate around, and, indeed, the state sought to reinforce the power of those structural constraints so that alternative pedagogies proved difficult to enact (an example in the United Kingdom is the way the state imposed a national curriculum and appropriate methods for teaching it by strengthening inspection, evaluation and assessment arrangements). Students also found it difficult to give voice to their own localised and immediately available experiential knowledge within the constraints of a formal curriculum and a formal process of schooling. The concentration on class, gender and race led to an essentialised, reductionist and, as a consequence, over-simplified view of identity formation; and the political ideals that underpinned critical pedagogy were frequently abstracted and decontextualised so that the movement itself lost impetus. Finally, critical pedagogy never developed beyond a system of ideas so that the relationship between culture and practice was never adequately operationalised.

To these problems and issues should be added the inability of critical pedagogy to confront the post-modern attack on foundationalism, both epistemological and, more importantly, ethical. In turn, critical pedagogy lost ground to technicist frameworks of understanding, which allowed governments round the world to set in place organisational and pedagogic structures antithetical to critical pedagogy.

Michael Apple's work (1979; 1982; see also Chapter 6 below) may be located within the field of critical pedagogy, and his focus has ranged from teacher education to school curriculum and national testing, to textbook production, educational financing and governance. In particular, he has been concerned to understand social reproduction, student socialisation, the hidden curriculum, inequality in all its various guises and curriculum knowledge. Like Apple, Henry Giroux's (1981; 1989; see also Chapter 10 below) work may be located within the field of critical pedagogy, and in particular the development of emancipatory citizenship. His later work embraces a post-modernist conception of knowledge, though he would still want to retain a version of ethical universalism.

Though Foucault's (1977; see also Chapter 5 below) work hardly touches on education and the curriculum, his general social theory has influenced and continues to influence discussions of the curriculum. His Nietzschian perspective is perhaps best expressed in *Discipline and Punish* (1977) in which he sets out to explain how technologies of power operate through new knowledge-power discourses and modes of objectification that individuals are subjected to and to which they subject themselves. His work on biopower and governmentality has direct implications for the study of the curriculum. All three of these key figures in the history of the curriculum have distanced their work from foundationalism and from economism, that is, in the first instance, adopting a universalist and trans-social view of knowledge, and in the second instance, understanding the aims and purposes of formal education as directly to produce trained workers for an efficient and effective economy, whether market-based or state-controlled. However, instrumentalism, as a curriculum form, has a number of different guises, and even critical pedagogy, underpinned as it is by a normative model of society, can be labelled as instrumentalist. Thus, in a broader context, instrumentalism has also come to be associated with any normative view of life as the end-point and purpose of formal schooling.

Instrumentalism

A different type of justification for the inclusion of items in a curriculum eschews foundationalism and epistemic conventionalism, and argues that it is possible to provide a justification for the contents of a curriculum in terms of certain virtues or experiences that children should have in order to lead a fulfilled life. The project is therefore clearly normative and redefines the notion of instrumentalism away from economism. It is a distinctive approach in that the curriculum is constructed in terms of whether the experiences undergone by students contribute to the development of dispositions that allow them to lead the good life. There are two principal problems with this approach: there is a difficulty with establishing what the 'good life' is; and there is an equal difficulty with identifying experiences for children in school which will lead to the development of dispositions so as to allow the individual to lead the good life when they leave school (cf. Callan, 1988; Clayton, 1993).

This further episode in the history of the curriculum therefore incorporates an idea of the good life as the end-point and indeed determinant of what should or should not be included in the curriculum. John White's abiding theme (1973; 1982; 1990; see also Chapter 12 below) has been that of autonomous well-being; he insists that the only way to resolve arguments about the curriculum is to define the good life and subsequently identify what the curriculum should be to give children the best chance of achieving it. His work has ranged from discourses about justice, altruism, work, lifelong learning and community to discussion of the philosophical rationale for a national curriculum. It is then his insistence on basing the curriculum round the notion of autonomy that marks out this particular curriculum episode, though in response to critiques of his early work he has refined and deepened this idea.

White (1982) argues for a notion of autonomy or the capacity to reflect on and make choices which allow the possibility of leading the good life and he suggests that if children do not develop such a capacity they cannot distinguish between projects which contribute towards the good life and projects which do not. Further, if they do not develop such a capacity, they are liable to be in thrall to arbitrary authority. Thus, the autonomous individual is treated as an ethical absolute, though again there are problems with identifying such an individual, because it is difficult to distinguish between actions which have been motivated by conformity to an arbitrary authority and actions that have genuinely resulted from the exercise of individual autonomy.

This dilemma for White reflects the tension between leading an autonomous life and a fulfilled one, and the two are not necessarily the same. Indeed, a person who indulges their appetites may not be considered to be autonomous, though clearly there is a sense in which they have chosen to indulge their appetites and have thus exercised their autonomy. It is here that the problem is at its starkest because autonomy as a concept cannot carry the weight attached to it, and there are implicit and normative meanings attached to it. So, autonomy means more than making choices or even having the capacity to make choices. There is a sense in which it is used to indicate the making of good or right choices and this is reflected in White's distinction between self-regarding reasons for choosing one form of life over another and other-regarding reasons in which a person also contributes to the welfare of others. Instrumentalist views of curriculum-making are future-orientated, and can therefore only be justified with reference to particular political and social arrangements. These arrangements, in turn, need to be argued for, and are likely to be contested.

School effectiveness/school improvement

Though it is important to separate out the two, academic theorists have sought to combine them, so that knowledge developed by school effectiveness researchers influences and indeed determines particular and prescriptive school improvement practices. This assumes a particular relationship between school effectiveness and school improvement, a technicist model which is at odds with critical, innovative and reflexive views of the curriculum. Indeed, what marks out this curriculum perspective is a neglect of the curriculum as such and an embeddedness in scientific models of curriculum-making. A typical prescriptive model that embraces both school effectiveness and school improvement discourses is provided by Pam Sammons and her colleagues.

Sammons *et al.* (1995) make the following claims:

- Although socio-economic factors and innate dispositions of students are major influences on achievement, schools 'in similar circumstances can achieve very different levels of educational progress' (1995, p. 83).
- There are some studies which suggest that both academic and social/affective outcomes such as attendance, attitudes and behaviour are determined by the school. In other words, children attended more, truanted less, had better attitudes towards schooling and behaved better whilst at school in the more effective schools compared with the less effective.
- Primary schools can have significant long-term effects on achievement at 16 years of age.
- It is possible to measure the difference which schools make. Creemers (1994, p. 13), for example, suggests that 'about 12 to 18 per cent of the variance in student outcomes can be explained by school and classroom factors when we take account of the background of students.'

- Prior achievement is a much more significant factor than gender, socio-economic, ethnicity and language characteristics, and even school effects are more important than these effects, but not that of prior attainment.
- There is some evidence that school effects vary for different kinds of outcomes, i.e. mathematical as compared with language achievements.
- The amount of variance in achievement attributable to schools and classes may vary from culture to culture.

These empirical findings are then translated into lists of interdependent factors that mark out an effective school from an ineffective one. Thus Sammons *et al.* (1995) produced a directory of effective school descriptors:

- professional leadership (firm and purposeful; a participative approach; the leading professional);
- shared vision and goals (unity of purpose; consistency of practice; collegiality and collaboration);
- a learning environment (an orderly atmosphere; an attractive working environment);
- concentration on teaching and learning (maximisation of learning time; academic emphasis; focus on achievement);
- purposeful teaching (efficient organisation; clarity of purpose; structured lessons; adaptive practice);
- high expectations (high expectations all round; communicating expectations; providing intellectual challenge);
- positive reinforcement (clear and firm discipline; feedback);
- monitoring progress (monitoring pupil performance; evaluating school performance);
- pupil rights and responsibilities (raising pupil self-esteem; positions of responsibility; control of work);
- home–school partnership (parental involvement in children's learning);
- a learning organisation (school-based staff development).

Here we have the scientific model of curriculum writ large, underpinned by technicist and managerial models of schooling; reductionist, tautological and in some cases trivial accounts of process; and more fundamentally, a distaste for many of the curriculum debates referred to above. However, these criticisms of this approach should not be used to underestimate the important effects this mode of curriculum-making has had in education systems round the world.

Curriculum models

These episodes or moments in the history of the curriculum, it should be reiterated, are not sequential, but overlap, reconstitute themselves in different guises and take on different forms in practice. The substantive argument of this book, as the last chapter will make clear, is to argue for a new model of curriculum, one which supports a conception of education as the public good. It therefore seeks to revisit some of the major curriculum issues that have surfaced since the mid-1970s with the intention of providing alternatives to the way that curriculum is now officially understood. It will do this by concentrating on some major themes as they have been expressed in the writings of key curriculum theorists. It will not therefore be a comprehensive exegesis of the work of each of these curriculum theorists. It will, however, seek to surface for the attention of the reader themes and issues that have both past currency and relevance to modern debates about education.

The structure of the book is as follows. This chapter has sought to provide the backdrop to the history of curriculum ideas by briefly examining some of the recent debates in relation to different models of curriculum-making. Chapter 2 examines a version of behavioural objectives advocated by W. J. Popham. Chapter 3 offers an opposing viewpoint and focuses on the work of Lawrence Stenhouse. In Chapter 4, reference is made to those important and influential curriculum models which are underpinned by foundationalist epistemologies, focusing in particular on the work of Paul Hirst. In Chapter 5 issues of relativism and power are addressed in relation to the writings of Michel Foucault. Chapter 6 concentrates on structural issues and, in particular, Michael Apple's distinctive view of educational systems, structures and curricular forms. Chapter 7 examines the influence of Basil Bernstein on pedagogy and in particular the relations between the different elements that make up the curriculum. Chapter 8 focuses on the learning process and Lev Vygotsky's internalisation thesis. The next three chapters address issues of reflection, critical pedagogy and psycho-cultural learning, taking as their critical lodestone three influential authors, Jerome Bruner, Henri Giroux and Donald Schon. The final author who is highlighted is John White, with his reflections on, and advocacy for, a notion of autonomy to underpin the curriculum. Finally, a different and post-modernist perspective on the curriculum is examined in the last chapter.

What then is a curriculum? A curriculum may refer to a system, as in a national curriculum; an institution, as in the school curriculum; or even to an individual school, as in the school geography curriculum. Its four dimensions are: aims or objectives, content or subject matter, methods or procedures, and evaluation or assessment. The first dimension refers to the reasons for including specific items in the curriculum and excluding others. The second dimension is content or subject matter and this refers to the knowledge, skills or dispositions which are implicit in the choice of items, and the way that they are arranged. Objectives may be understood as broad general justifications for including particular items and particular pedagogical processes in the curriculum; or as clearly defined and closely delineated outcomes or behaviours; or as a set of appropriate procedures or experiences. The third dimension is methods or procedures and this refers to pedagogy and is determined by choices made about the first two dimensions. The fourth dimension is assessment or evaluation and this refers to the means for determining whether the curriculum has been successfully implemented. This book offers a critical perspective on these various dimensions as they are addressed by the curriculum theorists identified above.

Chapter 2

Behavioural objectives and W. J. Popham

In his *An Evaluation Guidebook: A Set of Practical Guidelines for the Educational Evaluator* (1972), W. J. Popham argues strongly for a behavioural objectives model of teaching and learning, an approach that has had a considerable influence on the field of curriculum, culminating in the development of a national curriculum in the United Kingdom in the 1990s and similar policy initiatives round the world. Though educational theorists such as Popham embraced a technicist model of curriculum inherent in the specification of behavioural objectives, other curriculum theorists associated with this approach argued for weaker versions. Ralph Tyler (1950), for example, argued that specifying objectives was the only logical way of determining learning experiences. However, he did not subscribe to the view that they could be broken down into thousands of detailed educational sub-purposes, because he felt that this would unnecessarily restrict the teacher, and overwhelm their capacity to use them.

The rationale for developing this type of curriculum model was to provide clarity of purpose where none previously existed:

> The major advantages of such objectives is that they promote increased clarity regarding educational intents, whereas vague and unmeasurable objectives yield considerable ambiguity and, as a consequence, the possibility of many interpretations not only of what the objective means but, perhaps more importantly, whether it has been accomplished.
>
> (Popham, 1972, p. 31)

Behavioural objectives, for Popham, therefore have a number of features. First, they have to be unambiguously stated so that they provide explicit descriptions of the behaviours which should occur after instruction has taken place. These behaviours furthermore have to be stated so that any group of reasonable observers would agree that the individual concerned has shown themselves capable of performing them. Second, those behaviours have to refer to the learner and not the teacher. The teacher may devise systems of instruction which in themselves have merit; however, if they do not lead to the desired and pre-specified behaviours in learners, then they cannot be considered useful. Third, those behaviours should be expressed so that they can be measured; clarity is thus reduced to measurability. He therefore proposes that: 'The educational evaluator should encourage the use of instructional objectives which provide explicit descriptions of the post-instruction behaviour desired of learners' (1972, p. 33).

This is qualified by Popham to the extent that some objectives for instructional purposes are so intrinsically important that even if they cannot be measured they should still be included in the curriculum, for example aesthetic appreciation. However, he suggests that unmeasurable goals should not dominate the curriculum: 'We need to alter the proportion so that most of our goals are of a measurable nature, thus permitting us to determine whether they have been accomplished and, consequently, allowing us to get better at achieving them' (1972, p. 33).

Though he allows some licence for the teaching of unmeasurable goals for instructional purposes, he states quite explicitly that for evaluation purposes, unmeasurable goals are of no use. Thus, Popham's second proposition is that:

> While recognising that non-measurable goals will be of limited use for his [sic] purposes, the educational evaluator must be aware that instructors may wish to devote a reasonable proportion of their efforts to the pursuit of important but currently unassessable objectives.
>
> (1972, p. 35)

It should be noted here that Popham qualifies this acceptance of non-measurable goals with the suggestion that though currently they are non-assessable, they may be in the future.

Popham further explicates the differences between measurable and non-measurable goals by drawing a distinction between selecting from alternatives and constructing answers. He gives examples of each. In the first case the learner selects the true or false answer from a list of multiple-choice questions. In the second case, the learner constructs a response in the form of an essay, or a performance. In this latter case, for Popham, it is important that rather than relying on a general impression as to whether the learner is able to perform the action, criteria for adequacy are given so that it satisfies a group of judges. Again, he qualifies this, so that if the performance involves a number of criteria, those criteria should be so formulated that these judges should be able to determine, and agree amongst themselves, that the learner is able to fulfil a satisfactory proportion of those criteria. Thus Popham's third proposition in relation to behavioural objectives is that: 'The educational evaluator must identify criteria of adequacy when using instructional objectives which require constructed responses from learners' (1972, p. 39).

He is also concerned about the generality of content within the behavioural objective. He provides an example relating to the goal of understanding the narrative form of *Beowulf*, the epic tenth-century poem. The behavioural objective can be expressed either as the identification of three elements that characterise the epic form in *Beowulf*, or as three elements that characterise the epic form. Indeed, he argues that the most contentious issue with regard to the formulation of behavioural objectives is the degree to which they should be expressed as specific instances or general statements. Popham's strictures do not rule out the possibility of expressing such instructional objectives as relating to particular expressions of literary forms or the form itself, and the assumption that is being made by him is that the form is a relatively unambiguous and accepted item of knowledge. The distinction that he makes then is between content generality and test item equivalence and thus his fourth proposition allows for some measure of generality: 'The educational evaluator should foster the use of measurable objectives which possess content generality rather than test item equivalence' (1972, p. 40). In fact, Popham provides no guidance for determining whether objectives should be specific or general, but suggests only that instructors may prefer to work at a level of generality and thus this should not be ruled out.

Popham makes a further suggestion to the effect that behavioural objectives should take account of proficiency levels of performance, and that they should refer to either the individual learner or the class as a whole. Objectives therefore can be formulated so that they are only partially achieved, but this does not rule out their usefulness as curriculum tools. In line with the general thrust of Popham's argument, the suggestion is that a proportion of the objective can be achieved, whether by the individual or the class. The objective has therefore been met if nine out of ten members of the class can perform in a way that satisfies the criteria. He is equivocal about how these proportions should be worked out, and in the end leaves it to wise judgement, though he expresses this not in terms of political imperatives or drivers but in terms of insightful appraisal as to how learners should perform, taking into account both their previous performance and how they compare to other individual and age-related groups. Thus Popham's fifth injunction is that: 'Prior to the introduction of the instructional treatment educational evaluators should strive to establish minimal proficiency levels for instructional objectives' (1972, p. 40).

Popham further suggests that educational objectives need to be disaggregated according to the types of behaviours that they were designed to promote. Drawing on Bloom's *Taxonomy of Educational Objectives* with regard to cognition (Bloom and Krathwohl, 1956) and Krathwohl's *Taxonomy* in relation to the affective domain (Krathwohl *et al.*, 1964), Popham argues that curriculum-makers should use these to develop their lists of behavioural objectives. Three types of objectives are identified: the cognitive, the affective and the psychomotor. These in turn are broken down into six cognitive domains (knowledge, comprehension, application, analysis, synthesis and evaluation), five affective domains (receiving, responding, valuing, organising and characterising by a value or value complex), and five psychomotor domains (perception, set, guided response, mechanism and complex overt response). Thus Popham's sixth injunction is that: 'The educational evaluator will often find the Taxonomies of Educational Objectives useful both in describing instructional objectives under consideration and in generating new objectives' (1972, p. 44).

Popham's final piece of advice on writing objectives is that the curriculum-maker should borrow from existing banks of objectives to suit their needs. His last proposition is that: 'The educational evaluator should consider the possibility of selecting measurable objectives from extant collections of such objectives' (1972, p. 50).

Within this tightly defined system there are a number of propositions about curriculum knowledge that need to be examined. These relate to the nature of pedagogic knowledge and, in particular, to the reductionist form that the behavioural-objectives model implies; exclusions and inclusions within the knowledge corpus to fit the model; the purported value-free nature of the process that is advocated by behavioural objectives modellers; and the clear separation of means and ends in the system.

An epistemological critique of the model

A behavioural objectives model has to be operationalised, and, since the process involves the specification of observable performances and not inner states of being of the learner, behavioural indicators can only serve as approxi-mations of these inner states. Bloom *et al.* (1971, pp. 33–4), for example, argue that words which refer to those inner states are acceptable as general statements of intent, but then have to be broken down into performative behaviours:

> Thus while 'understands', 'appreciates', 'learns' and the like are perfectly good words that can be used in an initial, general statement of an objec-tive, they should be further clarified by the use of active or operational verbs that are not open to mis-interpretation.

The logic of their argument is that if words and phrases used in constructing objectives are clarified properly, then they can be translated into verifiable actions by the learner, so that the verification of those behaviours is not open to misinterpretation. Whereas it may seem that this follows directly from the need to clarify, in fact it introduces a new idea. The student behaviour that is being evaluated can only qualify as a proper objective if it is capable of being evaluated in an unequivocal way. This would seem to exclude the evaluation of a number of behaviours and therefore a number of inner states of the individual because any enactment of them is always open to interpretation as logically they can only be framed in this way. Some worthwhile educational activities are designed to be open to a number of interpretations, and thus within the strict boundaries of a behavioural objectives model these would have to be excluded. It is clear here that the model fits better certain types of activities than others; and thus to include all worthwhile activities will necessarily involve a distortion or packaging of some of them to fit the model. Examples of these might include the more expressive objectives of the curriculum.

There is a further problem with the atomised model of knowledge that is being proposed. A subject or discipline is broken down into its constituent parts which are then expressed in terms of behavioural objectives. Since this will consist of more and less difficult operations for the student to access, some order of these objectives has to be established, and this order comprises general principles for progression through a subject. In mathematics for example, this might consist of logically prior operations being taught which the student needs to be able to do before they can proceed to higher-level operations. The completion of one particular type of task entails mastery of a number of mathematical operations that precede it. The one cannot be performed without the other, and this is a logical way of understanding progression within a subject.

However, a distinction can be drawn between disciplinary knowledge and pedagogic knowledge, where this is understood as being between those logical connections and relations between different items of knowledge and the optimum way children actually learn (the enactment of pedagogic knowledge); and these two ways of ordering a disciplinary form of knowledge may conflict. In the first case a belief in logos is essential to sustain the character of the argument, and in the second case, a belief has to be sustained that there is an optimum way by which children should progress through a disciplinary structure. If, however, neither a belief in logos nor a belief in an optimum way of progressing through a discipline can be sustained, then progression as it is currently understood is merely conventional. If it is merely conventional, then it is open to being changed because it has no a-historical warrant. A behavioural objectives model with its atomistic implications implies some form of logical ordering between the different items, and this ignores the two other possibilities referred to above: an optimum or natural developmental process of learning and a conventional ordering without any foundation in either logic or psychology.

Dunne (1988), a critic of behavioural objectives, argues that there is no clear connection between teaching these atomised forms of knowledge and inculcating intellectual virtues which may be an important goal for the educator. The most appropriate way of inculcating intellectual virtues such as respect for truth, critical appreciation and the like is through processes and methods which do not reflect the behavioural objectives model of teaching and learning.

Dunne further questions whether a behavioural objective necessarily contains within it the unambiguous evidence for its verification. He points to the problem with a technicist language by definition precluding the need for interpretation, and the imperative of the behavioural objectives movement for unequivocal agreement that the behaviour being observed has been performed by the individual: 'This other assumption is what might be called practical verificationism – the stipulation that a well-formed statement of objectives must contain an indication of the evidence that would be required to verify whether or not it has been fulfilled' (1988, p. 67).

However, though this requirement was specified in the original model, a modified version is still logically coherent. Indeed, a modified version could be reconfigured as an objectives model, in which the links between inputs and outputs are considerably weakened, where these links refer to what is taught, how it is taught and what is learned. The OFSTED model in the UK is essentially of this type, since it involves a group of independent assessors observing teachers' and head teachers' behaviours at work, and then making an assessment as to whether and to what degree they meet a set of descriptors that are pre-specified by the body which is external to the school. Though this variant on the behavioural objectives model would seem to exclude the initial specification of objectives by the deliverer of the programme or by some other agency that compels that deliverer to operationalise these pre-specified objectives, what occurs in practice is that because the OFSTED inspection has attached to it a set of sanctions that if imposed have serious consequences for the institution being inspected, the teachers and head teacher within that institution rapidly conform to the behaviours specified in the evaluation protocol.

There is a further consequence: a behavioural objectives model in its most extreme form must specify those types of objectives that conform to the model and exclude those objectives that do not. And as I have suggested, this means that the objectives or purposes of a curriculum and the relative priority that is given to each of them is determined not by the criteria that a society develops as to the most appropriate and worthwhile items that should go in a curriculum, but by whether those objectives can fit a behavioural objectives model; or in other words, whether they can be specified in such detail, that, to use Dunne's term, they can be practically verified. I have already suggested that the objectives of a society as they are expressed in a school curriculum do not always take the same form. That is, some of these objectives can be better formulated within the model proposed by behavioural objectivists than others. For example, it is unlikely that expressive objectives can be formulated in such a way that an unambiguous view can be taken of whether the individual pupil can perform them. If such an unambiguous view can be given, it is likely that the expressive objective has been so formulated that it loses some of its force. As a result, there is a temptation to discard or marginalise objectives such as these, not because they are not worthwhile and thus should not form an essential part of the curriculum, but because they do not and cannot conform to the curriculum model being used.

Stenhouse (1975) in his seminal book, *An Introduction to Curriculum Research and Development*, offers other objections to the behavioural objectives form of knowledge. The first of these objections is that trivial learning behaviours may be prioritised at the expense of more important outcomes because they are easier to operationalise. As Stenhouse points out, the way this objection is framed can only be resolved by empirical investigation. However, there is a more profound point at issue, which is not directly addressed by the way this objection is framed, and this is that certain types of objectives can be framed in behavioural objectives terms (we may then want to call them trivial, but that is a different argument), whereas other types of objectives cannot be so framed. Thus concern for the spiritual well-being of pupils may be an entirely legitimate aspiration for a curriculum-maker, but determining whether at the end of a course of teaching this has been achieved is more difficult. In this particular case, it can only be framed as a guiding principle and not as a state of behaviour that can be identified after the event, however long after the event an attempt is made to identify it. However, there is a further part of the argument that we need to address: given that it is easier to express some objectives in behavioural terms and that these tend to be at a low level, then these will be prioritised at the expense of higher-level objectives simply because the latter cannot be expressed in simple identifiable terms. So, if a behavioural objectives model is adopted and there is pressure on teachers to teach to those objectives that can be measured in relatively simple ways, then these will be prioritised at the expense of those objectives which cannot be so measured. This is an argument that can be tested empirically. Galton *et al.* (2003) and Galton and MacBeath (2002) suggest that a deliberate narrowing of the primary school curriculum has occurred in the UK since the mid-1980s in response to the imposition by policy-makers of a behavioural objectives curriculum model, so that the school in general achieves a better position in the league table (in which schools' attainments in relation to specified targets are compared) with consequent losses in creativity and motivation.

Dunne makes a further point about such a specification. A behavioural objective has to be written at a general enough level so that an unequivocal judgement can be made as to whether it has been met. This presumes that the judgement being made is devoid of context, as consideration of context may not allow the behaviour being assessed to be unequivocally determined. The language used in the framing of the objective therefore has to be of a technicist nature, which means that the language itself has been stripped of all those elements that refer to context. In short, the language has to be decontextualised: 'What must be overcome, likewise, is any boundedness by particular contexts – any relativizing or qualifying to be done by users of this language in deference to a particular context in which it is used' (Dunne, 1988, p. 67).

Furthermore, this language has to be explicit, and a behavioural objectives model rules out not only context, but also the tacit element of language.

Delivering the curriculum

In this model, teaching is understood as the delivery of a set of pre-specified behavioural objectives which can be translated into observable behaviours and it is therefore positioned between the formulation of objectives and the evaluation of pupil behaviours after the event. The technical language therefore applies to this activity as much as it does to the input and output phases of the process. This approach turns the teacher into a technician, in the sense that a teacher cannot during the course of the encounter with the student speculate about the worth of the objectives or goals. These goals are pre-set, and thus context is ignored. One problem then is that the post-teaching evaluation can throw light only on the effectiveness of the teaching procedure rather than on the appropriateness of the objective or on what is being taught. A second objection is that the type of evidence demanded by the behavioural objectives model cannot provide any guidance as to how the teacher should modify their behaviour so as to produce better results. A behavioural objectives model that is underpinned by a taxonomic analysis of knowledge content does not take account of pedagogical knowledge or the way students learn.

With such a specification of the teacher–learner relationship, no account is taken of unintended effects. Since the purpose is effectively achieved if the learner can perform the clearly and explicitly stated action, the means to achieve this become irrelevant. So there is both an issue about unintended effects and an issue about the ethical consequences of arguing that any means are appropriate if the desired end is achieved. Means furthermore in this scenario are treated as ethically neutral since they do not figure as actions to be deemed ethical or not, but simply as actions which can only be judged to be ethically sound if the end-point of the process is achieved. Means are judged by criteria such as efficiency and effectiveness. Dunne (1988, p. 68) points out the following:

> I have been saying that these authors make a clear cut separation of ends and means, and deny any intrinsic purpose to means on the grounds that verified effectiveness in achieving given ends is the only relevant basis for selecting means (or 'methods'). No method, then, can, a priori, be either excluded or preferred to any other means.

Despite this clear separation of means and ends, governments in the United Kingdom have developed curricula within a behavioural objectives model, and at the same time intervened in the specification of means as well. Thus the logic of the behavioural objectives model has been commandeered to produce a performative model in which teachers are held accountable for both the production of good ends and the efficient following of means (teaching approaches) specified by outside bodies.

A further objection, made by Stenhouse (1975), is that pre-specifying explicit goals means that the teacher is rarely in a position to take advantage of unexpected instructional opportunities. As Stenhouse notes, this can only be tested empirically, but it would seem logical to suggest that teachers conscious of the need to meet the requirements of pre-specified goals will deliberately forgo other opportunities for learning even if they can see some benefit for their students. However, implicit within this argument is a further normative question, and this is whether it is appropriate for the teacher to forgo such learning opportunities, especially when they are also concerned to map the pre-specified curriculum to the developmental patterns of their students as they understand them.

Stenhouse argues that the teacher should be concerned not only with students' behavioural changes, but also with wider issues such as the ethical dimension of their behaviour, unexpected outcomes of adopting a rigid behavioural objectives regime, and the consequences of their behaviour on other stakeholders such as parents. This argument assumes that ends and means can be clearly separated, and that the efficient delivery of behavioural objectives can be achieved without the teacher paying any attention to unexpected consequences. A child can be forced to learn something and does so effectively; however, the means employed by which the child learns may have future consequences both for them as persons and for the subsequent absorption of that knowledge, which may in the end be harmful to that child.

Stenhouse further suggests that a behavioural objectives model denies the teacher that degree of independence from external bodies and in particular from governments that is needed if a free society is to be sustained and if a truly educated society is to be developed. For example, he argues that: 'classrooms cannot be bettered except through the agency of teachers: teachers must be critics of work in curriculum not docile agents' (Stenhouse, 1975, p. 75). Stenhouse's objections rest on a particular model of how teachers should behave, which is fundamentally in conflict with governmental notions of professionalism. For Stenhouse, there can be no proper curriculum development without the active engagement of the teacher. The teacher should not be understood as a technician, whose role is to deliver a pre-specified curriculum:

> Basically, the objectives approach is an attempt to improve practice by increasing clarity about ends. Even if it were logically justifiable in terms of knowledge – and it is not – there is a good case for claiming that it is not the way to improve practice. We do not teach people to jump higher by setting the bar higher, but by enabling them to criticise their present performance. It is process criteria which help the teacher to better his [*sic*] learning.
>
> (Stenhouse, 1975, p. 83)

In summary, the adoption of a behavioural objectives model implies that all worthwhile attainments can be measured at the end of the process of learning. However, some outcomes of education can only be reflected in behaviours which show up a long time after the teaching event and therefore cannot be expressed immediately. Second, some outcomes can more easily be expressed in behavioural terms and therefore it is likely that, if the teacher is under pressure to deliver a curriculum expressed in outcome terms, they will prioritise these objectives at the expense of those less amenable to measurement. Third, there is a temptation to express a particular objective in quantitative measurable terms and thus emphasise the quantitative aspects of the attribute, with a consequent diminution of its qualitative dimensions. The objective therefore becomes distorted. In the next chapter, Stenhouse's advocacy of a process model of curriculum development will be examined.

Chapter 3

Lawrence Stenhouse and the process curriculum

Lawrence Stenhouse died prematurely; had he lived he would have been dismayed by curriculum developments in the United Kingdom. He argued strongly against behavioural objectives as the cornerstone for the development of a curriculum. His arguments against such an approach are set out in his *An Introduction to Curriculum Research and Development* (1975), and are based on a belief in a form of inquiry learning related to and underpinned by knowledge developed in the disciplines.

We need to understand what is meant by his notion of *inquiry*. It is opposed to a didactic form of teaching where the student is presented with a version of knowledge developed in the disciplines, which they passively learn. Having been instructed in this way, the end-product is that the student now has this knowledge and if tested on it would be able to show that they have it. If there are gaps in that knowledge or if parts or wholes of that knowledge are misconceived, then a process of remediation takes place to correct the student's understanding. Disciplinary knowledge, for Stenhouse, however, cannot be adequately expressed in this form, and this is because a discipline is not a series of knowledge bites to be consumed by the learner, but a body of knowledge with its own logical structure and form or, as Schwab (1962, p. 14) called it, a syntax:

> This problem is hidden in the fact that if different sciences pursue knowledge of their respective subject matters by means of different conceptual frames, it is very likely that there will be major differences between one discipline and another in the way and in the extent to which it can verify knowledge. There is, then, the problem of determining for each discipline what it does by way of discovery and proof, what criteria it uses for measuring the quality of its data, how strictly it can apply canons of evidence, and in general, of determining the route or pathway by which the discipline moves from raw data through a longer or shorter process of interpretation to its conclusion.

Stenhouse described didacticism as a mode of learning which is concerned only with the superficialities of the discipline, and not with the syntax or underlying principles of the discipline or body of knowledge. Indeed, he strongly argued against the possibility and even appropriateness of teaching in a didactic way. However, if the student could be introduced to this syntax by being asked to take part in learning situations which embody these principles, even if in the first instance they are hidden or implicit, this would be of more benefit to the student than if they had been didactically instructed in them.

There are three problems with his approach. The first relates to the structure of disciplinary knowledge, and the second to the way knowledge is reconfigured at the pedagogic site. The third problem, however, is more fundamental, and this is that the non-didactic learning situation may be constructed so that the student acquires a false or misguided view of those principles or syntax (cf. Schwab, 1969; 1971; 1973; 1978). I will address each of these in turn.

A discipline seems to give us a reason for asserting that knowledge derived from it is true and thus should form the basis for what is taught in a curriculum. However, disciplines are organised groups of individual knowledge developers that evolve over time, and may be characterised in a number of interdependent ways. Knowledge within the discipline is tested against criteria developed by disciplinary practitioners, and therefore what constitutes evidence for assertions made by members of the discipline about its subject matter is influenced by the micro-political arrangements within the discipline.

A discipline, as I have suggested, evolves over time, with members of that discipline being replaced by other members, with some acquiring more power and influence than they had before and others losing status. Processes of replacement and displacement apply equally to current and to past members, some of whom are now dead or have retired from the field.

Further, a discipline cannot be understood as separate from other disciplines and may have strong or weak insulations between itself and other disciplines. In other words, the boundaries between disciplines are permeable, so that what constitutes the subject matter of the discipline, its epistemology and the criteria by which knowledge developed in the discipline is judged, change over time.

Disciplinary forms both reflect the way society is organised and in turn contribute to these social arrangements. Different disciplines are structured in different ways, so one discipline may have a knowledge base which is segmental, with weak insulations between these different segments, and, to use Bernstein's (1977, p. 167) phrase, comprising 'more and more specialised forms or languages'; another discipline, however, may be characterised by knowledge being arranged in a hierarchical fashion with an agreed and strong view of its epistemological warrant. What this suggests is that some disciplines can and should be understood not as unitary wholes but as competing sub-sets of individuals and groups, claiming legitimacy for their view of knowledge. Stenhouse's view of the legitimacy of disciplinary knowledge as a foundation for the curriculum therefore also needs to take account of the way such knowledge is developed in the first place; and indeed, at times he suggested that all knowledge is intrinsically problematic.

The second problem with basing a curriculum round the disciplines or representing the disciplines in the curriculum relates to how disciplinary knowledge is reconceptualised at the pedagogic site; in other words, disciplinary forms of knowledge are not transferred directly to the learning setting, but are pedagogically structured so that the knowledge developed in the disciplines is transformed as it is taught. This would suggest that a distinction needs to be drawn between disciplinary knowledge and pedagogic knowledge, and that any view of the curriculum needs to take account of this process of translation. Furthermore, if the discipline itself is characterised as: (a) having an evolving structure; (b) comprising a proliferation of languages; and/or (c) having a preferred epistemology, then each of these characteristics in turn is going to influence the type of translation that is undertaken and ultimately the form that pedagogic knowledge will take at the classroom level. The curriculum therefore comprises a principle of translation where a body of knowledge developed as a discipline undergoes a process of transformation as it is taught to students at whatever level of their development. School knowledge is different from discipline-based knowledge, and what follows from this is that given that there are different types of disciplinary knowledge, different pedagogic approaches, whether inquiry-based or didactic, may be appropriate.

The third problem relates to the likelihood that a student in the pedagogic encounter will misunderstand the syntax of the discipline. This may happen because it has been badly taught, or because the means of evaluation are such that a distorted version has to be taught to meet examination requirements, or because the student does not pay sufficient attention to the teaching of the discipline, or for a host of other reasons. The most immediate issue therefore is whether inquiry-based teaching or didactic teaching is more likely to result in the student grasping the essential syntax of the discipline. Since Stenhouse wants to suggest both that knowledge should be embedded in the disciplines and that the optimum means for acquiring this knowledge is inquiry-based, then this is central to his overall argument.

We are confronted here with an issue about what this syntax might be, even putting to one side the fact that it may be contested and that it may take a different form in the different disciplines. Stenhouse argues that:

> The superficialities of the disciplines may be taught by pure instruction, but the capacity to think within the disciplines can only be taught by inquiry. What is characteristic of the advocacy of inquiry-based teaching in this sense is the assertion that one can *think* in a discipline at elementary as well as advanced levels of study.
>
> (1975, p. 38)

History, for example, could be described as a set of procedures through which a historian operates; or as a body of facts about the past where there is general agreement amongst historians that these facts represent what happened; or as a series of explanations about the past that cohere in some specified way. If history is described as the former, a series of skills and dispositions that the historian has to acquire, then the inquiry method, regardless of whether the student provides right or wrong answers, would seem to allow an optimum translation between discipline and pedagogic setting. Indeed, one can go so far as to assert that the student is unlikely ever to learn these skills unless they have been allowed to behave as a historian, and literally practise those skills. On the other hand, if the end-point is that the student can reproduce the results of historical analysis, whether in the form of explanations of past events or as a series of facts which represent what happened, then it is more likely that the student will have acquired these explanations/facts if they are directly told what they are by a teacher and then given the opportunity to memorise them for the purposes of reproducing them in an examination or test.

We should note here that the skills required by the student for the successful execution of these processes cannot be subsumed into and do not represent the whole strata of skills required by the mature historian. Indeed, we may want to argue that the skill of memorising may actually be of little worth to the professional historian, and that therefore the student thus taught is ill equipped to act as a historian in the real world; or even that the student has acquired through practice a skill that may stand them in good stead in a general sense, but has little to do with being a historian, and the process of acquiring this skill makes it less rather than more likely that they will ever acquire the skills of being a historian. In this last case, they have literally been misled, and the translation has failed.

However, let us consider a further scenario, which is that this translation is more complicated than it seems. In the first instance, the student has to acquire the basics of a discipline before they can proceed to higher-level operations. This is not the logical form of the discipline, i.e. subtraction comes before multiplication in the discipline of mathematics, though it might be an important part of the syntax of a discipline; but it is the best order for a student to learn aspects of a discipline. If it could be shown that a student learns to become a historian in the first instance by being confronted with and learning the body of knowledge, those theories, explanations and descriptions of the past that historians have so far in the evolution of the discipline developed, even if this involves rote memorisation, then this would represent the best possible translation.

The argument in favour of this approach begins to look a bit threadbare at this point, for a number of reasons. The first is that it would seem more logical for a learning route to take the skills aspect first and then to allow the student to confront the theories and explanations produced by historians. The second is more serious, and this is that a linear route of learning, i.e. that one aspect of the discipline should be taught before another, may not be appropriate for all types of learners. Indeed, it is possible to suggest that what have come to be understood as appropriate routes of learning are not biologically programmed into the human psyche, nor even logically determined, but constructs developed by human beings in society, and these constructs themselves have implications not just for the way the learner learns, but also for how they understand themselves and how they behave in society. They are not and cannot be natural expressions of the process of learning. No amount of empirical investigation will solve this dilemma since all empirical investigation can do is find out how people learn and not how they could learn.

Given this, working out what the optimum translation might be is fraught with difficulties. However, we are now in a position to argue that didactic approaches favour one view of knowledge, and inquiry-based methods another. We can characterise these two views as polarities, though this in itself has certain dangers, principally that polarisation creates an either/or tension and thus marginalises any in-between position within the boundaries set by the two extremes. Didactic approaches make the assumption that learning is a process of absorbing a set body of knowledge which has the status of truthful versions of activities, processes and events in the world. The success or otherwise of the venture is determined by whether the student is able to reproduce this set body of knowledge and apply it without serious distortion in practical situations. No serious attempt is made to build into this pedagogic theory elements of assimilation, negotiation or interpretation. Inquiry-based approaches (and there are many variations on this theme) in general do not give as much credence to the reproductive nature of the process, but acknowledge that in the translation, the knowledge itself may undergo transformation. This means that if a student through discovery methods comes to the wrong conclusions, first they are not necessarily wrong and second it may not be important. As Elliott (1998, p. 29) comments, 'If what you want from the child is right answers, then informing them may be a more effective and efficient means of getting there than discovery learning.'

However, as I have suggested, the best learning environment may not necessarily be one in which the teacher wants the student to produce the right answers. There are a number of reasons for this. First, they value for their students the *process* of learning more than the *product*. Reasoning that school learning is inevitably a preparation for life, and we have to take seriously the notion of preparation both because the student is protected from the consequences of using their knowledge and because further educational experiences will allow the development and refinement of that knowledge and set of skills, the argument they make is that placing emphasis on process rather than product leads in the long term to a better-educated person. The child learns better, in other words, if they are allowed to make mistakes and are protected from the real-life consequences of making those mistakes, and if they learn from those mistakes by understanding why they made them. This is a different argument in favour of inquiry-based approaches because it emphasises appropriate pedagogy rather than appropriate reproduction.

In reality no teaching approach is likely to be purely didactic or purely inquiry-based. Indeed these are models which have logically distinct features. Stenhouse in turn accepts that one of these logical features, the type of knowledge that constitutes the discipline, varies between disciplines. Thus if we want to base our curriculum on the content and form of the disciplines, we have to take account of this:

> Instruction-based teaching implies that the task in hand is the teacher's passing on to his [sic] pupils knowledge or skills of which he is master. In discovery-based teaching the teacher introduces his pupils into situations so selected or devised that they embody in implicit or hidden form principles or knowledge which he wishes them to learn. Thus, Cuisenaire rods embody numerical principles. Instruction and discovery are appropriate in the classroom whenever the desirable outcome of teaching can be specified in some detail and is broadly the same for every pupil. Where a curriculum area is in a divergent, rather than in a convergent, field, i.e. where there is no simple correct or incorrect outcome, but rather an emphasis on the individual responses and judgements of the students, the case for an inquiry-based approach is at its strongest.
>
> (Stenhouse, 1967, p. 30)

Again Stenhouse confronts us with a set of polarities to understand the different epistemological bases of the disciplines and the implication is that a discipline may be more or less convergent or more or less divergent. We should also note his definitions of convergent and divergent. In the first case, convergency, there is a simple correct or incorrect outcome; in the second case, divergency, it is not just that there is no simple correct or incorrect outcome, the emphasis is a judgemental one made by the student. Stenhouse has moved here from an epistemological criterion about the discipline to a pedagogic observation about how students respond.

Inquiry-based pedagogy

A variant of inquiry-based pedagogy was espoused by Stenhouse in the 1980s. This culminated in the Humanities Curriculum Project, which concentrated on divergent disciplinary knowledge or knowledge developed through a divergent combination of disciplines. Here, I will concentrate on the principles that underpinned this method. The first of these is his well-known aversion to behavioural objectives and the replacement of these by a form of process objective.

> To abandon the support of behavioural objectives is to take on the task of finding some other means of translating aims into practice. We attempted

to analyse the implications of our aim by deriving from it a specification of use of materials and a teaching strategy consistent with the pursuit of the aim. In other words we concentrated on logical consistency between classroom process and aim, rather than between predetermined terminal behaviours and aim.

(Stenhouse, 1975, p. 89)

For Stenhouse,

Controversial issues are defined empirically as issues which do in fact divide people in society. Given divergence among students, parents and teachers, democratic principles are evoked to suggest that teachers may wish to ensure that they do not use their position of authority in the classroom to advance their own opinions or perspectives, and that the teaching process does not determine the outcome, opinions and perspectives of the students. It is important that there is no epistemological base to this argument. The position is that, given a dispute in society about the truth of a matter, the teacher in a compulsory school might wish to teach the dispute rather than the truth as he [sic] knows it.

(1975, p. 93)

And from this, he sets out a series of precepts for teaching these controversial issues:

1) that controversial issues should be handled in the classroom with adolescents;
2) that the teacher accepts the need to submit his [sic] teaching in controversial areas to the criterion of neutrality at this stage in their education, i.e. that he regards it as part of his responsibility not to promote his own view;
3) that the mode of enquiry in controversial areas should have discussion, rather than instruction, as its core;
4) that the discussion should protect divergence of view among participants, rather than attempt to achieve consensus;
5) that the teacher as chairman of the discussion should have responsibility for quality and standards in learning.

(Stenhouse, 1975, p. 94)

As evidence, carefully chosen texts, which represent the controversial areas of human endeavour, were presented to the students. The role of the teacher was to facilitate the discussion; thus rules about procedure were meant to be closely adhered to by the teacher, who acted as a neutral chairman, and whose role was to coordinate the discussion.

Furthermore, Stenhouse believed that the humanities require a hermeneutic process of understanding, where meaning resides not in the object of knowledge but in the process of interpretation. Elliott (1998) argues that this view of evidence as 'problematic knowledge' is embedded in a Gadamerian viewpoint, and it is worth examining the learning theory implicit in this.

The first part of the argument Gadamer (1975) makes is an epistemological one. Knowledge cannot be objectively known, where we define objectivity as implying a clear separation between the knower and what they are seeking to know. Learners bring to the learning setting their own beliefs, preconceptions and prejudices. However, he wants to rescue the term prejudice from its pejorative associations, and understand it as pre-judgement. All understandings for him are educative and have to be contextualised in terms of those pre-existing states (or pre-judgements) that are already a part of the learner's psyche. However, he is also concerned to emphasise that learners learn within familiar contexts but also have to make sense of the unfamiliar. The process of understanding therefore comprises the incorporation of the strange into the familiar, which has the effect of changing what is familiar so that in any future encounters the knower is positioned differently. For Gadamer (1975, p. 125), it is the tension between the strange and the familiar which contributes to the dialectic of learning about something:

> Hermeneutic work is based on a polarity of familiarity and strangeness. There is a tension. It is the play between the text's strangeness and familiarity to us, between being an historically intended, distanciated object and belonging to a tradition. The true locus of hermeneutics is this in-between.

The continuous interplay between *the whole*, which may be understood as the knower's worldview, and *the new*, that which is strange to the knower, is described as the hermeneutic circle. Though they are predisposed to see certain things in certain ways, this should not preclude them from understanding that these ways are continually undergoing transformation because of new encounters with the world. Their assumptions are therefore being continually challenged.

The second part of the argument that Elliott (1998) makes from a Gadamerian perspective concerns the optimum translation of this view of knowledge into principles of classroom practice. Despite Stenhouse (1975) holding a view that pedagogic knowledge should be underpinned by knowledge developed in the disciplines, he strongly believed that all knowledge was intrinsically problematic. It is the dialogic relationship between the knower and what they seek to know that for Stenhouse should be the real focus of the pedagogic encounter. The learner therefore is required in this process model to make their pre-judgements explicit or public, within a learning setting that approximates as far as possible to Habermas' (1987) view of the ideal speech situation.

Jurgen Habermas in his earlier work identified two important ideas. The first of these is what he called 'systematically distorted communication' (Habermas, 1987). Any claim to validity must be able to make the following assertions: what is being claimed is intelligible and meaningful; what is being asserted propositionally is true; what is being explained must be justified; and the maker of these claims must be sincere. The second notion he developed is the ideal speech situation. Agreement is possible between learners when it satisfies the criteria noted above and has been reached through critical discussion. In other words, it is agreement reached which is not based on custom, faith or coercion. These are very demanding conditions and it may be that Habermas' ideal speech situation should be understood as an aspirational rather than achievable end.

Stenhouse argued, then, for a learning setting that bypasses the normal power relations between teacher and student, and this would also comprise a bypassing of what he called the argumentative mode because though this allowed the presentation of the preconceptions and pre-judgements of the students, what it did not allow was any considered reflection, and therefore the possibility of their transformation. He saw the teacher's role as to protect a divergence of views and refrain from using their authority position to promote their own views. As Elliott (1998) points out, this should not be confused with promoting divergence, as this would involve the teacher in moving beyond the preconceptions and prejudices of the group of learners, and in effect imposing their view of the range of possible arguments on the learner.

The final stage of the argument is that the purpose of the exercise is to allow students to reflect on their own partially formed understandings (and in a sense all knowledge for Stenhouse was in a state of flux) in the light of other participants' alternative viewpoints. It therefore encouraged a more open, reflective attitude towards the judgements students made about matters of importance for the society in which they lived. The method also encouraged them to ask questions both of themselves and of other members of the group; and in particular to begin to reflect on the nature of evidence, understanding and learning. It could only be successful if the normal power relations that exist in the school setting were put to one side and the real question is whether it was possible to do this.

The extended professional

From this view of, and advocacy for, an inquiry-based method of delivery, comes a particular view of the teacher. For Stenhouse, the critical characteristics of the extended professional are: (a) a commitment to systematic questioning of their own teaching as a basis for development; (b) a commitment and the skills to study their own teaching; (c) a concern to question and to test theory in practice by the use of these skills; (d) a readiness to allow other teachers to observe their work – directly or through recordings – and to discuss it with them on an open and honest basis: 'In short, the outstanding characteristic of the extended professional is a capacity for autonomous professional self-development through systematic self-study, through the study of the work of teachers and through the testing of ideas by classroom research procedures' (Stenhouse, 1975, p. 144).

And thus was born the action research movement, though teachers in less systematic ways had been researching their classrooms since classrooms were invented. However, for Stenhouse, a number of conditions were necessary for this process to work. The teacher had to own the knowledge which they developed as a result of the process of action research. Ownership was necessary for two reasons: in order to effect change in the classroom, the teacher had to understand their own role in the process that they were researching and engage in a process of reflection about their own actions. In turn, this led to a process of reflection about the processes they were going through, with the intention of finding solutions to problems in their classroom and solving them. As Stenhouse argued, this process which gives primacy to the practitioner's own understandings can never be complete without some form of externalisation. This took the form of studying other teachers and allowing them to provide an alternative viewpoint to the practitioner's own practice. However, this cannot be subsumed into a model of professional development where the practitioner is required to set aside their own preconceptions and knowledge of themselves and their practice and replace it with a model of behaviour that has been developed through objective study of classroom processes and teacher behaviours. The practitioner builds on their own knowledge of what they are doing by seeking other perspectives and by absorbing these other perspectives into their own knowledge of their practice, and in the process they develop or grow as teachers.

It is to be noted that Stenhouse's model of teacher development mirrors the process of learning that he advocated for student learning. It does this in a number of ways. First, knowledge is always provisional, even if that knowledge has been codified as disciplinary knowledge: thus knowledge of how teachers should behave in the classroom cannot be subsumed into a science of pedagogy; it is always emergent and context-based. Second, knowledge of their own practice evolves and develops as their understanding deepens. However, the process is more complicated than this, because the internal conversation that they have drives the learner in particular ways. Learning is not just about a passive absorption of what is given to consciousness, but an active process which leads to action in the world or, in the case we are considering, the classroom. Thus problem-solving both solves problems and reframes the knower so that in future encounters they experience the world in different ways and indeed experience those problems in different ways. Third, Stenhouse advocates learning taking place, whether for student or teacher, as a community affair, that is, with other people engaged on similar types of activities.

There can be no curriculum development, as Stenhouse so cogently argued, without teacher development.

> Idea and action are fused in practice. Self-improvement comes in escaping from the idea that the way to virtuosity is the imitation of others – pastiche – to the realisation that it is the fusion of idea and action in one's own performance to the point where each can be 'justified' in the sense that it is fully expressive of the other. So the idea is tuned to the form of the art and the form used to express the idea. Thus in art ideas are tested in form by practice, exploration and interpretation lead to revision and adjustment of idea and of practice. If my words are inadequate, look at the sketchbook of a good artist, a play in rehearsal, a jazz quartet working together. That, I am arguing, is what good teaching is like. It is not like routine engineering or routine management. The process of developing the art of the artist is always associated with change in ideas and practice. An artist becomes stereotyped or derelict when he ceases to develop. There is no mastery, always aspiration. And the aspiration is about ideas – content – as well as about performance and execution of ideas.
>
> (Stenhouse, 1975, p. 65)

In this chapter, two important curriculum themes have been highlighted: relationships between disciplinary and pedagogic knowledge, and the viability of inquiry-based learning. Stenhouse has implicitly, though at times reluctantly, moved away from a foundationalist view of knowledge to structure the curriculum. In the next chapter, I will examine the work of Paul Hirst who formally adopted, certainly in the first instance, a foundationalist view of curriculum knowledge.

Chapter 4

Paul Hirst and foundationalism

Typical of philosophers of education writing in the 1980s was Paul Hirst, with his designation of the curriculum as an initiation into forms of knowledge or cognitive structures. It matters little for the purposes at hand that Hirst later revised the number and type of forms. What is important is that Hirst's philosophy represents an attempt to base the contents of the curriculum round a theory of mind which enabled him to distinguish between different logical forms of human thinking:

> the development of the mind has been marked by the progressive differentiation in human consciousness of some seven or eight distinguishable cognitive structures, each of which involves the making of a distinctive form of reasoned judgement and is, therefore, a unique expression of man's rationality.
>
> (Hirst, 1969, p. 242)

We are therefore immediately confronted with two different versions of the logos. The first of these comprises a generic theory of mind, based on a belief in the inherent rationality of human beings, or at least in their capacity to act rationally. The rational person is someone who is able to access the logos; the irrational person violates it. The second version that Hirst argues for is domain-specific, so that within this theory of mind there are a number of sub-categories, each of which has its own form of logic, and criteria for determining the truthfulness or otherwise of propositions relating to the domain. In the first instance, he identifies seven domains: logico-mathematical, empirical, interpersonal, moral, aesthetic, religious and philosophical (Hirst, 1974a; 1974b). As he argues, 'these would seem to me to be logically distinct areas, though this division might well be disputed' (Hirst, 1969, p. 243).

He acknowledges that forms of knowledge take on different guises and are labelled differently, but suggests that these new forms of knowledge are iterations of old ones. They have their place in the development of knowledge, but these new iterations do not constitute new forms of knowledge with their own distinctive logical characteristics:

I see no a priori reason whatever why new forms of knowledge should not arise. But there is, I think, little positive reason to think that this in fact is what is happening. What there is in abundance now, are new interdisciplinary areas of study in which different forms of knowledge are focused on some particular interest, and because of the relations between the forms, what is understood in each discipline is thereby deepened. Such new areas of study do not constitute new areas on the map of knowledge based on the logical distinctions I have mentioned. They are essentially composite, second-order constructions, not to be confused with the primary forms of knowledge which I have distinguished on logical grounds. In terms of these primary forms of knowledge, the new areas seem to be exhaustively analysable.

(Hirst, 1969, p. 151)

He further argues that there is a logical relationship between the form of the knowledge domain and the way it should be taught. In other words, curriculum delineations are made in terms of the different types of logic espoused by the various disciplines and it is these different types of logical form which are predisposed to a particular type of instruction or pedagogy. The example he gives relates to progression within the forms, since in some cases certain items of content logically precede other items of content, with the latter not being able to be properly understood without knowledge of the former, e.g. mathematics.

Since understanding the structure of knowledge domains is fundamental to a proper education, to deny such a comprehensive initiation into these forms to some groups of learners, on the grounds that they are too hard for them, or that since they will not be useful to them in later life they do not need such an initiation, is to misunderstand the nature of a liberal education, which is by definition inclusive:

If the objectives of our education differ for sections of our society so as to ignore any of these elements for some of our pupils, either because they are too difficult, or for some reason they are thought less important for these pupils, then we are denying to them certain basic ways of rational development and we have indeed got inequality of educational opportunity of the most far reaching kind.

(Hirst, 1969, p. 151)

This foundationalist view of knowledge can be challenged in two ways. In the first place, there is no evidence to suggest that the theory of mind espoused by Hirst is anything other than an expression of how human beings have in the past divided up knowledge; indeed, to provide a transcendental reason for such a foundationalist view of knowledge would involve a claim about our capacity to know what the logos is. This is not provided by Hirst;

indeed, what he suggests is that the development of the human mind has been progressively differentiated so that it now embraces a number of logically distinct cognitive structures, the implication being that these cognitive structures are simply the result of the mind's evolution as it responds to changing cultural conditions, and that therefore such structures could have been different. It should be noted, however, that Hirst is in effect 'naturalising' his curriculum rationale by asserting that even though the human mind has evolved, this is how human beings currently are constituted. The second way his foundationalist view of knowledge can be challenged is by examining his proposition that though these distinctive cognitive structures are all expressions of rationality, even if they each have their own logical structure, nevertheless these structures are sub-sets of a wider sense of rationality or logos. Hirst has been criticised for suggesting that all his forms of knowledge are different expressions of the logos, whereas some of them at least seem to have no direct relationship to it.

Hirst distinguishes between the forms in four ways. Each of the forms has a number of concepts and ideas attached to it, which the initiate or learner has to understand in the precise way that they are used by members of the discipline. For example, a religious form has a particular understanding of the concept of a deity. These concepts and ideas are understood as existing in a particular relationship to each other so that experience is made sense of, and this network of relationships which are particular to each form, therefore has, in Hirst's terms, a distinctive logical structure. Thus the discipline of history has a different logical structure from the physical sciences and the one cannot be understood by using the concepts and logical structure of the other. Each discipline or form has developed particular ways of testing its knowledge against experience: 'Each form, then, has distinctive expressions that are testable against experience in accordance with particular criteria that are peculiar to the form' (Hirst, 1972, p. 15). Finally, allied to this, is that each form has developed particular skills and techniques, which are different in the forms by virtue of their particular logical structures; and Hirst suggests that there are both distinctive disciplines or forms of knowledge, and fields of knowledge such as theoretical and practical arenas in which knowledge is both developed and applied.

What allows one to claim objectivity for knowledge, and thus provide a sound rationale for structuring the curriculum, is that each of these forms of knowledge has publicly verified criteria for their warrant:

> For it is a necessary feature of knowledge as such that there be public criteria whereby the true is distinguishable from the false, the good from the bad, the right from the wrong. It is the existence of these criteria which gives objectivity to knowledge; and this in its turn gives objectivity to the concept of liberal education.
>
> (Hirst, 1972, p. 14)

A foundationalist view of knowledge, then, is underpinned by a realist ontology, a belief that this knowledge inheres in the world regardless of how it is received and interpreted by individual human beings, and a belief that the world can be known in an objective way. The curriculum therefore has to reflect these foundations of knowledge, and learners have to be initiated into an understanding which embraces them. A liberal education then is a rite of passage through which a student goes, so that at the end of the process the learner has grasped the forms or structures which inhere in intrinsically worthwhile knowledge forms. Furthermore, if a learner for whatever reason is not initiated in this way, then they can be said both not to be fully educated and not to have the capacity to make authentic choices and thus not to have developed as an autonomous being.

Two objections can be raised to this view of knowledge and thus of the contents of the curriculum. The first is that the development of the disciplines, indeed the development of distinctive forms of knowledge and distinctive public tests and criteria for distinguishing between them, are located in historical struggles between groups of people. In short, the results of such struggles could have been different from what they are. Thus, Hirst's first version of objectivity – knowledge is objective if it conforms to certain public tests of verifiability – is a limited form of objectivity in that it goes no further than conventionalism. His second version of objectivity is different, though he does not clearly distinguish between the two and this is his defence of metaphysical and epistemological realism. Approving of a platonic conception of knowledge, he argues that the fully developed Greek notion of liberal education

> asserted that the mind, in the right use of reason, comes to know the essential nature of things and can apprehend what is ultimately real and immutable. Consequently man [*sic*] no longer needs to live in terms of deceptive appearances and doubtful opinions and beliefs. All his experiences, life and thought can be given shape and perspective by what is finally true, by knowledge that corresponds to what is ultimately real.
>
> (Hirst, 1972, p. 2)

This second version of objectivity is a much stronger version in that it asserts that there is a true version of reality and that through careful deliberation and investigation it is possible to know what it is, since knowledge of it can in some way correspond to it. This point of view in effect rules out a number of well-known epistemological positions: radical relativism, where it is asserted that there is no reality in itself but only a way of going on in life; conventionalism, where it is asserted that true and certain knowledge of reality is unobtainable but human beings have developed particular forms of knowing which constitute reality; perspectivism, where it is suggested that reality though influencing descriptions of it cannot determine what those descriptions are, and thus multiple perspectives are possible, equally valid, and incommensurable; and critical realism, which emphasises ontological emergence and at the same time epistemological transience.

A foundationalist view of knowledge, and therefore of the appropriate contents of the curriculum, has in the twentieth century been dealt a series of epistemological blows to the effect that few now believe that the building of such foundations is possible. A distinction needs to be made between correspondence and irrealist views of the world. With the former, a mirror image of the world is suggested whereby knowledge of the world, mediated through language, reflects in all its essentials the world as it is. Thus the curriculum can be thought of as a reflection of this real world, and if this view is challenged, proponents of it can argue that this is a significantly better way of proceeding than one which is based on an unreal view of the world. Initiation into an unreal view of the world cannot therefore be justified at all, and indeed no such rationale is ever attempted. What is disputed is the existence of such foundations and furthermore the ability of human beings to access such foundations. In short, it is the relationship between knowing the world and reality itself which is placed under the microscope.

Such challenges to this foundationalist view of epistemology came in the form of critiques by philosophers such as Quine (1953) who argued that the relationship between ontology and epistemology is never as straightforward as the mirror image assumes. Observations of the world are conceptually mediated, in that all observations involve prior theorisation and therefore cannot be thought of as theory-independent. Facts about the world are only facts in so far as a prior definition of what a fact might be is provided. So a curriculum that is justified on the grounds that its contents comprise facts about the world which cannot be disputed by any rational person is inadequate in that this misrepresents the ontology of the world. A further distinction needs to be made here and this is between theory-dependence and theory-determination. In the latter case, no empirical examination of the world is necessary because the world itself can be read off from a prior theoretical framework. In the former case, theory precedes observation, but does not determine the contents of those observational statements. These are in a methodological sense independent of them. Further to this, Quine sought to dissolve the long-standing distinction between analytic categories and synthetic categories. Analytic categories are understood as definitional; synthetic categories are observational statements grounded in and tested against experience. For Quine, there can be no definitional truths that we can know absolutely without them being understood as in the world and thus subject to the changing forms of that world; and likewise there can be no empirical truths grounded in experience which are independent of a prior theory. The collapse of this distinction also had profound implications for the distinction Hirst drew between mathematical and empirical forms of knowledge, since each of Hirst's forms was so constructed as to have a distinctive logical structure. If that logical structure for each one of the forms is shown to be shared with other forms, then it is harder to argue that there are a determinate number of independent forms.

Structuralism

However, though philosophers have generally accepted that naive realist views of ontology and epistemology are not viable, they have not abandoned beliefs in realism and embraced conventionalist and relativist alternatives. A further attempt to develop a foundationalist epistemology surfaced in the emergence of structuralism. Carr (1998) describes how foundationalism can be reinserted through a belief in the necessary ordering of human experience. This notion of natural necessity is central to any foundationalist view of the curriculum and Carr argues that following Kant, there are limits to the way human beings can access the world:

> However, in the manner of their main enlightenment inspiration Kant (1968) – structuralists were inclined to believe that the basic categories of human thought and language disclose something in the way of a necessary ordering of human experience; thus, beneath the surface grammatical differences which distinguish particular cultural forms of thought and language there is – in terms of Chomskian linguistics – a 'deep grammar' (Chomsky, 1965) that reflects the way in which experience would have to be conceptualised to be the object of human knowledge at all.
>
> (Carr, 1998, pp. 9–10)

Strawson (1959) had previously argued for some universals of coherent thought that would set limits to those forms of life that individuals are embedded within and to the way those individuals can and do process reality. This solution, however, cannot provide us with any certainty about what those universals might be, since it is the universals themselves that are implicated in the process of their own identification. However, if we put this to one side, structuralist arguments provide a possible way out for the foundationalist curriculum developer, since by virtue of their logical structure, they seek to exclude other possible ways of understanding the world in favour of one which might be called a correct view of epistemology, and this therefore provides sufficient justification for structuring the curriculum in foundational terms.

The most prominent form that structuralism took was the linguistic variety and in particular the belief that it is the hidden and underlying structures of language that condition the behaviour of individuals. Furthermore, those linguistic structures are common to human beings, regardless of their situation, geographical positioning or cultural ethos. Thus structuralism opens itself up to being criticised for ethnocentricism, as these structuring forms are usually described in terms of individuation, rationality or complexes of western values. Structuralism itself gave way to post-structuralism, and Carr (1998, p. 10) identifies the principles behind such a programme:

> In a nutshell, post-structuralists are inclined to deny what structuralists uphold – that there are universal, ahistorical and transcultural concepts or categories of human thought and understanding lurking beneath the diverse socio-culturally conditioned forms of thought, speech or discourse encountered by field psychologists, anthropologists or linguists.

Hirst's search for an epistemological foundation to knowledge, providing a bedrock for the curriculum, has been subverted by new understandings of knowledge and in some cases by anti-epistemological positions (cf. Rorty, 1979). However, curriculum theorists have not abandoned all hope of providing an epistemological justification for the curriculum, as we will see.

Conventionalism

Conventionalists provide an alternative viewpoint to foundationalism, because they argue that epistemology is rooted in human affairs. The contents of the curriculum are the results of careful and systematic deliberation through history of the development of knowledge in disciplinary forms, and though these disciplinary forms are fluid configurations, such a position avoids relativism, and allows curriculum developers a base from which they can construct the contents and form that a curriculum should take. For a conventionalist, reality is mind-independent, but epistemologically no sense can be made of the proposition that human beings can know reality in any absolute sense. Furthermore, there is the possibility of describing reality in a number of different ways; however, this is limited by the ways individuals and groups of individuals have chosen in the past, and are currently choosing, particular and specific ways of understanding the world. They posit a two-way relationship between reality and conceptual framework, so that reality influences framework and, likewise, framework influences reality. They are opposed to solipsistic views of the world, because they argue that individuals cannot create the world in any way they want, but can only do so in terms of conventions established by other people, which constitute reality, and from which a curriculum can be constructed. Conventionalists therefore argue that the network of ideas and concepts that mediate reality are the result of past and current power struggles by knowledge-creating and knowledge-disseminating agencies, and their resolution, partial but never complete, results in conventions about how reality is mediated.

The issue of relativism is taken up by Moore and Young (2001) with particular reference to the curriculum in their article 'Knowledge and the Curriculum in the Sociology of Education: Towards a Reconceptualisation'. It is worth considering their argument here. For them, the curriculum debate has been structured in terms of two competing traditions; the first of these is what they call 'neo-conservative traditionalism' and the second is 'technical-instrumentalism'. Neo-conservative traditionalism represents the curriculum as a given body of knowledge that should be preserved through its institutionalising in schools. Pedagogy is understood as contemplation of the canonical texts that constitute the various disciplinary traditions. The emphasis is on a respect for tradition and authority, expressed through a particular view of knowledge. Technical-instrumentalism is fundamentally opposed to this view of knowledge. Technical instrumentalists are concerned to construct the curriculum around the needs of the economy. For them, the curriculum is understood as a means to an end, the end being a successful, efficient and competitive knowledge-based economy. The dispositions that education is meant to nurture are flexibility, entrepreneurship, trainability and a willingness to take part in a market economy. Whereas previously vocationalism was reflected in a work-related, practically orientated curriculum for those who were not considered to be academic, more recently the technical-instrumentalist curriculum has embraced employability for all students. Moore and Young (2001, p. 451) also suggest that this viewpoint is congruent with 'a style of managerial regulation that is integrated with the broader apparatus of performance indicators, target setting and league tables', and this chimes with Foucault's notion of technologies of the self.

The next stage in their argument is to suggest that critiques of both of these positions end up by treating curriculum content as arbitrary and furthermore as perpetuating social inequalities. These critiques, basically of a postmodern persuasion, start from an assumption that knowledge is embedded in particular interest perspectives, and thus conceal those interests under the guise of a spurious objectivity. The implication for the curriculum is that epistemologically its contents are bound to be arbitrary (since post-modernists do not accept any foundational principles that underpin knowledge), but that in effect the knowledge base of the curriculum is so constructed that some groups in society are disadvantaged and others advantaged. It is here that the argument has to confront the difficult issue of relativism. For if knowledge is essentially arbitrary, then all knowledge is determined by social and political arrangements; or to use Foucauldian terminology, power and knowledge are inseparable. This is a conclusion that Moore and Young are not prepared to accept. For post-modernists, there are no absolute grounds for determining that particular areas of knowledge should be curricularised and others not.

Moore and Young then proceed to argue against this position and their resolution of the debate is crucial to understanding whether a view of knowledge can prevail that should underpin the curriculum. Their first argument is that post-modernists polarise and trivialise the two positions, neo-conservatism and technical-instrumentalism. The neo-conservative position then is not just about preserving an arbitrary standard, but also about understanding education as an end in itself and thus placing knowledge as central to any discussion of the curriculum; second, though it may preserve entrenched and partial interest positions, it is also crucial for maintaining and developing standards and conditions for the development of new knowledge. For Moore and Young, their disagreement with this position rests on the tendency of the neo-conservatives to reify knowledge developed in the past and thus ignore the way knowledge evolves in response to changing conditions and innovation. In like fashion, instrumentalism is criticised because it prioritises economism at the expense of all other worthwhile justifications for education and, second, it does not address the proper conditions for new knowledge.

It is the second argument that they make against post-modernism that goes to the heart of their thesis. Post-modernism implies relativism and therefore arbitrariness; the denial, in other words, that knowledge can be objective. The implication is that if knowledge can be shown to be objective, then this provides the basis for determining what should be included in the curriculum and what should not. For them, it is the very social nature of knowledge that provides good grounds for objectivity. In support of this argument, they quote Alexander (1995, p. 91), and it is worth citing it here because it goes to the kernel of their argument:

> Either knowledge . . . is unrelated to the social position and intellectual interests of the knower, in which case general theory and universal knowledge are viable, or knowledge is affected by its relation to the knower, in which case relativistic and particularistic knowledge can be the only result. This is a true dilemma because it presents a choice between two equally unpalatable alternatives. The alternative to positivistic theory is not resigned relativism and the alternative to relativism is not positivistic theory. Theoretical knowledge can never be anything other than the socially rooted efforts of historical agents. But this social character does not negate the possibility of developing either generalised categories or increasingly disciplined, impersonal and critical modes of evaluation.

Knowledge for Alexander, then, and for Moore and Young (2001) is being redefined so as to preclude accusations that it is relativistic in character. Knowledge cannot be rooted in universalistic and trans-social categories but is constructed by historical agents, operating within determinate historical periods, and therefore our present version of knowledge has evolved from the efforts of many human agents, some long since dead. This is a different argument from the one which suggests that all knowledge is rooted in particular interests because the suggestion is that particular interests are presently constructed, but knowledge, though it may have been constructed originally by particular human agents with particular interests, has this enduring quality which may (though does not always) transcend the particular interests of present-day agents. Independent criteria are literally independent of standpoints and should not be equated with them. As Moore and Young argue, some knowledge can transcend the immediate conditions of its production. They therefore posit three arguments: first, knowledge is intrinsically social and collective; second, intellectual fields implicated in the construction of new knowledge are characterised by a complexity that post-modernists reduce to power relations; and third, there is an asymmetry between cognitive and other interests and the two should and cannot be equated. Power and knowledge in Foucauldian terms therefore are not inextricably tied together; and it is possible to understand and develop the latter without reference to the former.

Ultimately, this is not a convincing argument, for a number of reasons. The argument rests on the possibility of distinguishing between those forms of knowledge which are interest-bound and those forms of knowledge which transcend the interests of human agents. However, to determine which is which demands a form of reasoning which transcends both the historical genesis of the particular and presently conceived idea of knowledge, and more importantly the past conception of knowledge which has provided the grounds for Moore and Young to argue that some types of knowledge can be objective. In order to show that knowledge is objective, it is necessary to argue not just that the form of knowledge transcends the particular interests and circumstances of the particular knowledge constructor, but more importantly that the criteria for determining whether this is true or false, good or bad, accurate or inaccurate knowledge are not rooted in social arrangements made by human agents, but are transcendental. The argument that Moore and Young have advanced simply moves our definition of objectivity to embrace the social and the historical, and yet classical definitions of relativism do just this. Their argument is based on attacking a straw man – post-modernists, such as Foucault, would accept the social nature of the categories that underpin knowledge.

Since the criteria for determining the verifiability of knowledge not only are but were based on human arrangements and therefore are historically relative, this replaces a strong version of objectivity with a much weaker version, and suggests that since knowledge is based on convention, and since the justification for including certain items of knowledge in the curriculum and excluding others is likewise based on the development of knowledge in the disciplines, then such knowledge forms could be different from what they are. Conventionalism acknowledges that there are no transcendental justifications for knowledge, and opens the door to the assertion made by Foucault (1977) and others that knowledge and power have a closer relationship than is generally acknowledged and that certain forms of knowledge which become dominant have consequences for the way society is organised and may contribute to forms of inequality and oppression which some curriculum theorists (cf. Giroux, 1997) would seek to change.

Chapter 5

Michel Foucault and power-knowledge

In the previous chapter, I discussed a foundationalist view of knowledge, which curriculum theorists in the 1980s found particularly attractive. Michel Foucault, arguing from a different standpoint, developed a relativist view of knowledge (cf. Taylor, 1998), in which power and knowledge are inextricably related. Modernist curriculum thinkers, such as Lawrence Stenhouse and Jerome Bruner, argued that knowledge needs to have its roots in the disciplines and that pedagogic knowledge at its best reflects the optimum translation of this knowledge into the curriculum. For Foucault, this transcendental move to provide a foundationalist view of the curriculum is misguided in that it is not possible to have any certainty about the correctness or otherwise of how the curriculum should be constructed. Foucault understood the disciplines as discursive formations, as having no foundational status, and as being embedded in history.

Olssen (2004, p. 64) offers a Foucauldian view of the disciplines:

> In methodological terms, the central key to understanding the disciplines as discursive formations is as structures 1) which manifest definite rules and regularities; 2) where these rules and regularities are compatible with the episteme of the age in the sense of establishing limits and exclusions, and are affected by the practical constraints of institutional power and control within the social structure; 3) which determine and limit the conditions of possibility, i.e. what it is possible and legitimate to say and write, what counts as reason, argument, or evidence; 4) which are autonomous in the sense that they do not integrally represent being; 5) which are anonymous in the sense that they are not linked to or embodied in individual subjects but are themselves, ontologically, part of a discursive regularity; 6) which go through transformations and experience radical discontinuities at particular periods which are sharp but not complete; 7) which constitute forms of power that shape subjects and assist in the regulation of social life through the process of *normalisation*.

A number of key themes and ideas can be generated from this view of disciplinary knowledge. Foucault breaks with structuralism in that disciplinary knowledge is embedded in history and constitutes a particular type of historical configuration. If structuralism is understood as a form of theory in which underlying structural forces in society not only condition but determine the forms of thought, beliefs and actions of individuals, and as determinative of the human condition per se – for example, human beings are embedded in language structures which allow them to think in a particular way, and exclude other ways of thinking – then Foucault breaks with structuralism. But this is only in so far as he builds into the model a notion of how disciplines are embedded in history and cannot provide any transcendental view of knowledge. In short, they are historical products.

Furthermore, relations between power and knowledge, for Foucault, take a particular trajectory. Liberal and Marxist versions of power are described as having the following features. First, power is possessed at different levels or strata of society, so the state can exercise power in terms of its capacity to impose sanctions on individuals, for example through the judicial system; and individuals can impose power on other people again through the exercise of sanctions and punishments. Second, power is always exercised from the top downwards and thus society is hierarchically arranged with those at the top having the capability of exercising more power than those at the bottom. Third, power is always repressive, in the sense that it prevents individuals from doing certain things. For Foucault, power is exercised and not possessed as such; power is productive as well as repressive; and power does not necessarily flow from the top to the bottom in society but may work in reverse (cf. Sawicki, 1991, pp. 20–1).

A number of points need to be made about Foucault's conception of power and his suggestion that power relations in society should be characterised as a 'multiplicity of force relations' (Olssen, 2004, p. 63). The first of these is that though power undoubtedly flows throughout networks of human relations, it can also be exercised by powerful people by virtue of their role or position over less powerful people. It is not only that the individual exercises power in relation to other people and institutions, but also that this individual exercises power through their position in society and through their capacity to impose sanctions on other people. Some people can force other people to do certain things that they perhaps do not want to do. Foucault would, I am sure, have had no problem with this. However, what he wanted to suggest was a more inclusive view of power, which cannot replace in its entirety liberal and Marxist views of power, but which is at one and the same time repressive and productive. To separate out productive power from repression renders the whole notion of power redundant.

Productive power is then fundamentally concerned with disciplinary knowledge. 'There is no power relation without the correlative constitution of the field of knowledge, nor at the same time any knowledge that does not presuppose and constitute at the same time power relations' (Foucault, 1977, p. 27).

Historically, the study of and justification for the curriculum has focused on the issue of knowledge and it is here that Foucault's particular view of knowledge is relevant. For Foucault, knowledge has a particular relationship with power and indeed is inextricably linked with it. This, however, has been interpreted in a number of different ways, both relativist and universal. Olssen *et al.* (2004), for example, argue that Foucault did not want to suggest that there are no universal truths, and use this passage from his 'Preface' to the *History of Sexuality*, Volume 2, to support their argument.

> Singular forms of experience may perfectly well harbour universal structures; they may well not be independent from the concrete determinations of social existence. However, neither these determinations nor these structures can allow for experiences. . . . Except through thought. . . . This thought has an historicity which is proper to it. That it should have this historicity does not mean it is deprived of all universal form, but instead that the putting into play of these universal forms is itself historical.
>
> (Foucault, 1984, p. 335)

What Foucault is suggesting here is that the expression of any universal truth, in a curriculum for example, takes a particular form which is historically specific, and it is the determination of these forms that is of concern to curriculum theorists. This would seem to mirror MacIntyre's (1988) notion of a tradition. For MacIntyre, within any historical moment there may be dominant traditions of thought, rival traditions which demand less allegiance and traditions which are going through epistemological crises. But these traditions cannot be subsumed under one notion of rationality. They are incommensurable, though it is possible to observe another tradition from a different perspective. As MacIntyre (1988, p. 356) himself argues, this means that 'we either have to speak as protagonists of one contending party or fall silent'. These traditions compete with each other as they imply different and conflicting notions of rationality. If they did not, then they would not strictly speaking be different. There would, in other words, only be right and wrong ways of seeing the world: 'but genuinely to adopt the standpoint of a tradition thereby commits one to its view of what is true or false and, in so committing one, prohibits one from adopting any rival standpoints' (MacIntyre, 1988, p. 367). It is not that one party is more or less correct than another, or that members of one tradition understand rationality better than members of another tradition. Rival traditions are genuinely in competition with each other and cannot within their own way of life reach an agreement. That they may do so occurs because one or other of the parties has abandoned wholly or in part those precepts which constituted the tradition to which they formerly belonged.

If we accept MacIntyre's version of rival and competing traditions, then we are forced down the path of both judgemental and epistemic relativism. Foucault, however, still wants to draw a distinction between universal criteria for truth (and this would avoid the pitfalls of relativism) and the form that this truth takes which is always historically specific, and thus the form truth takes is always relative to particular versions of human life and is therefore located in society. His way out of the dilemma is to suggest that the theorist is concerned with the forms that they take and that these forms should be judged by their own criteria, but these forms are located within universal structures, even though the theorist can only observe the form from a particular standpoint. If these forms of knowledge are creations of particular societies, then they are also the product of particular power struggles that have taken place in the past and are currently taking place; and to make a particularly Foucauldian point, the construction of these forms of knowledge also determines the conditions under which future struggles about knowledge will take place. There is thus a dialectical relationship between knowledge and power. Knowledge structures create power arrangements, and in turn and in different ways power arrangements form knowledge structures. However, because Foucault is determined not to offer us a simple relativist view of knowledge, he is forced to accept a distinction between the creation of knowledge and how it can be justified. A truth may be produced because of certain arrangements in society (this would refer to issues of access, availability, dissemination, suppression, obfuscation, etc.), but its ultimate truth value is not determined by or dependent on any of these but is established through a universal principle of rationality. Ultimately, this is not convincing, given the close relationship that Foucault wants to establish between power and knowledge.

Relativism and the curriculum

Why then is the issue of relativism important for the study of the curriculum? We first need to distinguish between the different forms of relativism. In the philosophical literature four types of relativism are discussed. The first of these is moral relativism. This is where there are no universal grounds for suggesting that one version of morality is superior to another. This is supported by the fact that moral systems vary across cultures, historical periods and different people within the same culture. It would be false to infer from this that there are no moral absolutes, as one of those systems might be right and all the others wrong. However, in the absence of other arguments to the contrary, this would suggest, but not prove conclusively, that there are no moral absolutes. Again, there is no suggestion here that moral relativists should be entirely sceptical about the existence of moral absolutes, though perhaps this gives them good grounds for being sceptical about identifying what they might be. Even if most societies or indeed every society shared some moral belief, this in turn would not prove the existence of moral absolutes, since all of them might be wrong. Furthermore, moral relativists might claim an allegiance to a moral system, which is embedded in the society to which they belong, without at the same time subscribing to any absolute or universal system of morality.

The second type of relativism is conceptual relativism. Different people in different cultures and in different time periods vary in the way they organise experience. They therefore operate with different conceptual frameworks. As with moral relativism, the argument of variety does not disprove the existence of some universal conceptual system by which reality can best be known. However, it is more difficult to believe in conceptual relativism than it is to believe in moral relativism, because whereas the one is concerned with behaviours and right actions, the other is concerned with accessing the world. A conceptual relativist would argue that thought, belief and knowledge systems are embedded in particular social arrangements, which cannot be changed through individual willpower, but nevertheless do not persist over time and are different in different cultures. Immersion in one culture means that it is only with the greatest effort, if at all, that a person can access another culture, and even then, they are stepping outside their native culture and entering a new one. The two cultures are still incommensurable.

The third type is perceptual relativism. This is a sub-set of conceptual relativism, and the same dilemma applies here as with the first two categories. Whorf (1954, p. 213) defines perceptual relativism in the following way:

> We dissect nature along lines laid down by our native language. The categories and types that we isolate from the world of phenomena we do not find there because they stare every observer in the face; on the contrary, the world is presented in a kaleidoscopic flux of impressions which has to be organised by our minds – and this means largely by the linguistic systems in our minds.

Perceptual or radical relativists argue that there is no grounding in nature that compels us to organise it in one way rather than another.

The fourth type is truth relativism. Radical relativists would argue that there are no universal absolutes embedded in logic or rationality. Different societies have their own systems of logic, their own sets of criteria for determining the truth of the matter, and their own procedures for carrying this out. To understand another culture, therefore, requires a complete reappraisal of how one thinks and therefore how one behaves.

A number of objections to these various forms of relativism has been noted. There is a logical objection to epistemic relativism. Since relativism denotes a universality, i.e. that all knowledge is relative to the values of the knower, or the disciplinary matrix in which the researcher is embedded, or social, geographical and political arrangements, then it undermines itself, since this implies a universal statement which is denied by the substance of the argument.

Furthermore, there is an evidential objection to relativism. Though judgements between statements about reality are difficult to make, it is possible to discriminate between sound evidence and unsound evidence, and this evidence provides the means by which such judgements can be made. This argument against relativism acknowledges that judgements that are made are based on criteria which are developed in communities, but it is only through activities which underpin such communities, i.e. peer review, that such criteria can be developed and used.

There is a moral objection to relativism. If all values, including values about apt or false research accounts, are located in historical and social arrangements, then there is no way of effectively choosing one version over another, and this leads to an 'anything goes' thesis or an anarchic view of the world.

Finally, there are a number of conceptual objections to epistemic relativism. It is contrasted in an absolute way with a definitive account of reality; this creates a dichotomy between the two states which does not allow the possibility of a middle position; and furthermore, if a middle position was allowed, then this position would have to be defined in terms of its polar extremes. Relativism at one end of the continuum is contrasted with a concept at the other end which is not the opposite of it – a false comparison is made – and further to this, the one extreme cannot be defined in opposition to what it is not, except in so far as it trivialises it.

All these different forms of relativism are essentially anti-realist, though more moderate relativists suggest that the world can be real even if there are no absolute or universal standards by which it can be judged. Thus reality exerts an influence on the way it is described which means that it cannot be described in every possible way. Indeed, as we have seen, some philosophers (cf. Strawson, 1959) have even suggested that there are some universals of coherent thought, which would set limits to those forms of life that individuals are embedded within and the way those individuals can process reality.

As we saw in the previous chapter, attempts have been made to anchor knowledge in the disciplines and thus avoid these forms of relativism. For example, Hirst (1974b) proposed that the curriculum should be structured in terms of distinctions made between the forms of knowledge. These disciplined forms of knowledge may be distinguished in a number of ways. Each discipline has developed a set of concepts that organises experiences and thoughts in particular ways. In religious studies emphasis is given to a notion of spirituality which depends on a metaphysical notion of God. In physics, concepts such as atom and molecule have been developed to explain the physical world. Each discipline has its own form of determining truth from falsehood; scientists use processes of observation and testing to determine the truth value of a theory; mathematical statements, on the other hand, are true by reason of the logical rules that constitute the system in which they work. Thus each discipline can be distinguished by epistemological criteria for how statements of truth and falsehood are verified. Disciplines therefore are not just differentiated through these epistemological criteria, but also through a rejection of the tenets of another discipline. So some physicists would want to argue that metaphysical speculation, the central tenet of theology, is an illegitimate standard to use in evaluating human affairs. Thus disciplines compete by offering rival versions of epistemology. The techniques and methods that have been developed by practitioners are different in each discipline and act as markers for distinguishing one discipline from another. So, the historian has been inducted into a particular way of understanding, collecting and collating evidence that may be significantly different from the experimental methods adopted by scientists. Finally, practitioners within the various disciplines draw boundaries round their activities, and specify the type of problems that they set out to solve. Notwithstanding these differences between the forms, they are all considered to be expressions of a universal notion of rationality.

Foucault was not convinced by this, and despite his specific denial, ultimately grounds rationality in socio-cultural and historical contexts. This means that the distinction he wants to make between judgemental and epistemic rationality is an illegitimate one. Disciplinary knowledge comprises forms of rationality which evolve through different epistemes so that individuals see the world in different ways in different time periods and places. His concern is to describe the emergence of different forms of knowledge that literally make possible genetics (Foucault, 1970), for example, or statistics (Hacking, 1999), or madness (Foucault, 1977) or confession (Foucault, 1978). It is the rules of the specific and historically located discursive formations and complexes of them which constitute what can or cannot be included in a curriculum.

Categories and delineations

Foucault's notion of power-knowledge and discourse, and his relativist take on the issue, place a question mark against naturalism, a key theme of Henri Giroux's work. And what he means by naturalism is the idea that since discursive regularities are historically embedded, then the way those discourses are constructed has a profound effect on how we can think, what counts as evidence in argument and ultimately what should and should not be included in the curriculum in schools. Naturalism can be thought of both as a reasoned argument for the curriculum, in the sense that particular dispositions and ways of thinking are natural to human beings living in different societies and in different time periods, and as a rhetorical device for affirming one set of curriculum specifications over another. It works by constructing sets of categories, the relations between them, and practices that flow from them as the norm, and in the process radically repositions individuals in society.

An example of this classifying process is the use of the notion of intelligence, and in particular the idea of a fixed innate quality in human beings which can be measured and remains relatively stable throughout an individual's life. This has come to be known as an intelligence quotient (IQ) and is measured by various forms of testing, e.g. the 11+ test. The 11+ had a significant influence on the formation of the tripartite system of formal education in the United Kingdom as it was used to classify children as appropriate for grammar schools (those who passed the 11+), technical schools (those who passed the 11+ but were considered to be better suited to receive a particularly focused technical education), and secondary moderns (the vast majority who failed the 11+ and in the early days of the tripartite system left school without any formal qualifications).

Central to the concept of the intelligence quotient is the tension between the relative emphasis given to genetically inherited characteristics and the influence of the environment, or the 'nature versus nurture' debate. Many contemporary educationalists believe that children's early and continuing experiences at home and at school constitute the most significant influence on their intellectual achievement. However, early exponents of the argument that genetic inheritance determined intellectual potential saw intelligence, measured by tests, as the factor which could be isolated to produce a 'quotient' by which individuals could be classified. Regardless of environmental factors such as teaching and learning programmes or socio-economic variables, it was argued, some people were born with low levels of intelligence. Schooling could bring them to a certain level of achievement, but there would always be a genetically imposed ceiling on their capabilities. An extreme version of this belief was that intelligence, like certain physical characteristics, followed a normal curve of distribution, so that within any given population there were a set number of intelligent people and a set number of less intelligent people. It was further argued that those individuals who were most generously endowed were obviously more fitted to govern and take decisions on behalf of those who were less fortunate.

The use of IQ tests was widely accepted as a selective device among academics and the writers of government reports, including, for example, the Spens Report (1938) and the Norwood Report (1943), both of which influenced the writing of the United Kingdom Education Act of 1944. The 1944 Education Act incorporated the beliefs, first, that intelligence testing could reliably predict who would succeed academically at a later point in time, and second that children could and should be divided into categories based on the results and educated separately.

Soon after the 1944 Act was passed, the use of IQ tests to allocate places began to be discredited. One of the appeals of the policy was its supposed objectivity and reliability. If intelligence was innate and could be measured, then the tests would simply reflect this notionally 'pure' relationship, but this is not what happened. A number of other problems with this idealised concept became apparent. IQ tests should by definition be criterion referenced. If children had the intelligence, the theory went, then the tests would show it. All children who demonstrated their intelligence by achieving the designated mark ought to be awarded a place at a grammar school. In practice, Local

Education Authorities set quotas for grammar school entrance. Furthermore, different Local Education Authorities set different quotas for passing (Vernon, 1957). The quotas also discriminated against girls. The argument was frequently made that since girls developed earlier than boys in their intellectual abilities, fewer girls should be given places in grammar schools because this would unfairly discriminate against boys who would catch up later.

A second problem with IQ tests was that if intelligence, as measured by the tests, was innate, then coaching and practice ought not to improve pupils' test scores. However, it was reported that pupils' performances were indeed enhanced by preparation for the tests, demonstrating that a supposedly free-standing assessment was being connected to the curriculum in contradiction to the intentions which lay behind it (Yates and Pidgeon, 1957). More importantly, Yates and Pidgeon's findings threw into question the notion of an innate and immutable intelligence quotient. Finally, the deterministic beliefs underlying the system implied low academic expectations for pupils who failed the 11+. A low IQ score at age 11 ought to be a reliable guide to the rest of their school careers. However, it quickly became apparent that some of those who failed were capable of achieving high-level academic success.

This complicated story illustrates one of the problems with the reification of categories and delineations between them. What was considered to reside in the nature of reality, i.e. innate qualities of intelligence in human beings, was shown to have undeniably social or constructed dimensions to it. Communities of individuals had constructed a powerful tool for organising educational provision, and given it credibility by suggesting that it was natural and thus legitimate.

This view of the changing nature of discursive formations implies that new ways of describing the social world are always operating and replacing old ways, even if those new ways are in a critical relationship to the old. If this is accepted, then curriculum-makers are not entitled to say that there are stable and enduring relationships in society that constitute reality, which is independent of them. They can only say that those stable and enduring relationships are constituted as stable and enduring because of the historical play of signifiers that constitutes their understanding of the social world, which in turn impacts on historically located but evolving human practices; and this applies equally to the methods that they use to examine the nature of that social world. This position is neither solipsistic nor naively realist, but it does acknowledge the time-specific nature of their deliberations about the world. What it also implies is that as curriculum-makers they cannot avoid entering into a critical relationship with previous and current ways of describing the world and since the way they create knowledge is a part of that social world, entering into a relationship with reality itself and possibly changing it (the internal critique). Therefore essentialising explanations, i.e. the production of generalisations that persist across time, are approximations to existing conditions that currently pertain.

Foucault and the examination

I have provided one example of the construction of a discursive formation. Foucault provides another in relation to the use and development of examinations. In *Discipline and Punish: The Birth of the Prison* (Foucault, 1977), Foucault surfaces the commonsense discourse which surrounds examinations by showing how they could be understood in a different way. Previously, the examination was thought of as a progressive mechanism for combating nepotism, favouritism and arbitrariness, and for contributing to the more efficient working of society. The examination was considered to be a reliable and valid way for choosing the appropriate members of a population for the most important roles in society. As part of the procedure, a whole apparatus or technology was constructed that was intended to legitimise it. This psychometric framework, though continually in a state of flux, has served as a means of support for significant educational programmes in the twentieth century, i.e. the establishment of the tripartite system in the United Kingdom after the Second World War, and it continues to underpin educational reforms since the passing of the Education Reform Act for England and Wales in 1987. Though purporting to be a scientific discourse, the theory itself is buttressed by a number of unexamined principles: a particular view of competence; a notion of hierarchy; a way of understanding human nature and a correspondence idea of truth. Furthermore, the idea of the examination is firmly located within a discourse of progression: society is progressively becoming a better place because scientific understanding gives us a more accurate picture of how the world works.

In contrast, for Foucault (1977, p. 184) the examination:

> combines the techniques of an observing hierarchy and those of a normalizing judgement. It is a normalizing gaze, a surveillance that makes it possible to qualify, to classify and to punish. It establishes over individuals a visibility through which one differentiates them and judges them.

The examination therefore does not just describe what is, but allows society to construct individuals in certain ways and in the process organises itself. Knowledge of persons is thus created in particular ways which have the effect of binding individuals to each other, embedding those individuals in networks of power and sustaining mechanisms of surveillance which are all the more powerful because they work by allowing individuals to police themselves. The examination, according to Foucault, introduced a whole new mechanism which both contributed to a new type of knowledge formation and constructed a new network of power, all the more persuasive once it had become established throughout society.

This mechanism worked in three ways: (a) by transforming 'the economy of visibility into the exercise of power' (1977, p. 187); (b) by introducing 'individuality into the field of documentation' (1977, p. 189); and (c) by making 'each individual a "case"' (1977, p. 191). In the first instance, disciplinary power is exercised invisibly and this contrasts with the way power networks in the past operated visibly, through perhaps the naked exercise of force. This invisibility works by imposing on subjects a notion of objectivity which acts to bind examined persons to a truth about that examination, a truth which is hard to resist. The examined person understands him or herself in terms of criteria which underpin that process, not least those of success or failure. The examination therefore works by 'arranging objects' (1977, p. 187) or people in society. In the second instance, the examination allows the individual to be archived by being inscribed in a variety of documents which fix and capture them. Furthermore, it is possible to understand this process even when the rhetoric of what is being implemented is progressive and benign. Since the mid-1980s in English and Welsh schools, the proliferation and extension of assessment through such devices as key stage tests, records of achievement, examined course work, education certificates and school reports *and* evaluation through such devices as school inspection, teacher appraisal, profiles and the like mean that teachers and students are increasingly subject to disciplinary regimes of individual measurement and assessment which have the further effect of fixing them as cases. The third of Foucault's modalities then is when the individual becomes an object for a branch of knowledge:

> The case is no longer, as in casuistry or jurisprudence, a set of circumstances, defining an act and capable of modifying the application of a rule; it is the individual as he [*sic*] may be described, judged, measured, compared with others, in his very individuality; and it is also the individual who has to be trained or corrected, classified, normalized, excluded, etc.
>
> (1977, p. 191)

One final point needs to be made about the examination, as Foucault understands it, and this is that for the first time the individual could be scientifically and objectively categorised and characterised through a modality of power where difference becomes the most relevant factor.

Hierarchical normalisation becomes the dominant way of organising society. Foucault is suggesting here that the examination itself, a seemingly neutral device, acts to position the person being examined in a discourse of normality, so that for them to understand themselves in any other way is to understand themselves as abnormal and even as unnatural. This positioning works to close off the possibility for the examinee of seeing themselves in any other way. Policy texts work in the same way. The reader is not just presented with an argument and then asked to make up their mind about its merits or demerits, but positioned within a discourse – a way of understanding relations within the world – which, if it is successful, restricts and constrains the reader from understanding the world in any other way. This discourse is characterised as common sense, whereas in fact it is merely one way of viewing the world and is therefore ideological.

A concern with Foucault's work is that he is offering a structuralist view of the world in which individual agency becomes a pale shadow of its real self. This theme will be taken up in the next chapter, which examines, through the eyes of Michael Apple, structural constraints and enablements on pupils, teachers and schools.

Chapter 6

Michael Apple on structure

Michael Apple, in his extensive writings, has focused on various structures that have impacted on school curricula; however, he has consistently taken the position that educational actors are able, and have the capacity to, resist these structural influences. He therefore distances his work from deterministic and structuralist views of reality. Porpora (1998) suggests that structure has been given four distinct meanings. The first of these is 'patterns of aggregate behaviour that are stable over time'; the second is 'law-like regularities that govern the behaviour of social facts'; the third is 'systems of human relationships among social positions' (1998, p. 339); and the fourth is, following Giddens (1984), 'collective rules and resources that structure behaviour' (Porpora, 1998, p. 339).

The first of these is what has been called *methodologically individualist* – social structures are understood as abstractions built up over time and developed from systematic observations of behaviours. Methodological individualism, as a social theory, has been criticised because it marginalises structural properties, so that structures are treated as though they have no causal influence on human behaviours. Critical realists, in contrast, allocate independent powers to structure and agency, whereas methodological individualists deny such powers to structures, and thus make redundant the separation of agency and structure.

The second of Porpora's versions of structure is *law-like regularities that govern the behaviour of social facts*. In reverse fashion, no attempt is made to integrate the different levels of social reality, and this marginalises the intentional dimension of human action. As Archer (1995) suggests, this has the effect of treating these law-like regularities as operating behind the backs of human actors, and subsequently reifying objects in the world with the consequence that their powers and potentialities become redundant. Social facts which refer to pre-existent structural forms and do not make reference to intentional behaviours cannot logically be construed as nomological because those structural forms are always subject to change as a result of interpretations and mediations by individuals and groups of individuals.

The third of Porpora's models of structure, *human relations among social positions*, prioritises relations between human beings, so that agency and structure operate in a dialectical manner, with both exerting an influence on the other, because both have independent powers. Porpora (1998, p. 344), for example, argues that:

> [t]he causal effects of the structure on individuals are manifested in certain structured interests, resources, powers, constraints and predicaments that are built into each position by the web of relationships. These comprise the material circumstances in which people must act and which motivate them to act in certain ways. As they do so, they alter the relationships that bind them in both intended and unintended ways.

Giddens' (1984) *structuration model* – Porpora's fourth version of structure – suggests that structures only have a virtual existence and is idealist in that they are located exclusively in the minds of individuals. Structures may work in this way, and discourses have real causal powers; however, realists would argue that structures are independent of individual minds. Both of these versions, Porpora's third and fourth models, avoid methodological individualism and structural determinism, and are thus to be preferred at the ontological level.

Michael Apple's work has focused on the enduring power of the state and the structural activity that it can command by virtue of its control of both material and ideological apparatuses in society. We will see how he has consistently avoided Porpora's first two versions of structure, by emphasising the power and potentiality of agency to check untrammelled state control. This has direct implications for how the curriculum in schools has been and can be constructed, and moves the debate from justifications for knowledge structures to the politics of curriculum implementation.

State power

Apple's position is that relations between the state and the education system should not be construed as one-way with the former exerting a binding influence on the latter.

> The educational system is not an instrument of the capitalist class. It is the product of conflict between the dominant and the dominated. The struggle in the production sector, for example, affects schools, just as it conditions all state apparatuses. Furthermore, because the State, including the educational system, is itself the political arena, schools are part of social conflict. Education is at once the result of contradictions and the source of new contradictions. It is an arena of conflict over the production of knowledge, ideology, and employment, a place where social movements try to meet their needs and business attempts to reproduce its hegemony.
> (Apple, 1982, p. 50)

Apple's work attempts to illuminate the relationship between the state, civil society and the education system. His early work expressed a profound dissatisfaction with deterministic and typically Marxist theories (cf. Bowles and Gintis, 1976), which denied any independence for the education system from the class-determined form that capitalist society took. This economistic and functionalist position did not allow for any form of resistance to structural forces in society and, in its functionalist variant, understood the education system as part of a perfectly functioning system in which all the different parts, including the education system, worked in harmony to reproduce a capitalist society. This theory of society has been heavily criticised: for its structuralist implications (i.e. hidden structures and powers constitute the life of a society and agents are the unwitting recipients of such structures and cannot in any real way influence them); for its inability to account for change within society (i.e. since the whole structure relegates agents to the periphery, the only form of change that can occur is through the working out of contradictions at the structural level); and for its denial of agency (i.e. it maintains that agents have causal powers, whilst at the same time it acknowledges that structures in turn have causal powers).

Apple (1982, p. 2) in his earlier work was clearly dissatisfied with such a view of the relationship between society and the education system:

> Others, especially Bowles and Gintis, have focused on schools in a way which stresses the economic role of educational institutions. Mobility, selection, the reproduction of the division of labor, and other outcomes, hence, become the prime foci for their analysis. Conscious economic manipulation by those in power is often seen as a determining element. While this is certainly important, to say the least, it gives only one side of the picture. The economistic position provides a less adequate appraisal of the way these outcomes are created by the school. It cannot illuminate fully what the mechanisms of domination are and how they work in the day-to-day activity of school life. Furthermore, we must complement an economic analysis with an approach that leans more heavily on a cultural and ideological orientation if we are completely to understand the complex ways social, economic, and political tensions and contradictions are 'mediated' in the concrete practices of educators as they go about their business in schools. The focus, then, should also be on the ideological and cultural mediations which exist between the material conditions of an unequal society and the formation of the consciousness of the individuals in that society. Thus, I want here to look at the relationship between economic and cultural domination, at what we take as given, that seems to produce 'naturally' some of the outcomes partly described by those who have focused on the political economy of education.

The position he expresses here has been the driving force for his later work. There are a number of elements that need to be emphasised. The first is that an economistic view has been moderated by an emphasis on culture and ideology which, for Apple, allows some independence between the two. He is not immediately rejecting the notion that a person's classed position is reinforced by the education system; however, he is introducing a further element into the dynamic, which is that ideological or cultural formations also have a part to play in the formation of society. Two relationships are therefore foregrounded: between the economic and cultural systems; and between these structures (both material and cultural) and the consciousness of agents.

How and why do oppressed agents take on forms of consciousness which contribute to their own oppression?

> All too much of this kind of neo-Marxist scholarship treated the school as something of a black box and I was just as dissatisfied with this as I was with the dominant tradition in education. It did not get inside the school to find out how reproduction went on. In many ways, oddly, it was an analogue of the Tyler rationale in curriculum, in that the focus tended to be scientistic and to place its emphasis on input and output, consensus, and efficient production. The interpretations placed upon the school were clearly different from those of Tyler and the efficiency minded curriculum 'experts', yet schools were still seen as taking an input (students) and efficiently processing them (through a hidden curriculum) and turning them into agents for an unequal and highly stratified labour force (output). Thus, the school's major role was in the teaching of an ideological consciousness that helped reproduce the division of labour in society. This was fine as far as it went, but it still had two problems. How was this accomplished? Was that all schools did?
>
> (Apple, 1995, p. 28)

Thus schools needed to be interrogated as to how the various processes work. They should not be treated as merely peripheral to class-based explanations of society. If they are, this creates a number of problems, common to many structuralist versions of society. These can be summarised as the dilemma of reproduction/transformation theories, which deny the powers of agency and marginalise the possibility of resistance to structural imperatives.

For Apple, the relationship between structure and agency has to be understood in historical terms, and in a similar fashion structural formations have to be understood as a result of historical struggles. They could, therefore, have had different outcomes. Furthermore, though a particular arrangement of structural forces has resulted, such an arrangement can be contested and is thus open to replacement by a different settlement. Though class relations expressed in terms of the material forms of economic production in society are singularly resistant to change, cultural forces are less resistant, and through sustained action – an example of which is Apple's work itself – can be transformed. An individual's class position can be overcome through transformation at the cultural level, which may operate in two ways. First, it can transform the material base of society and thus subvert the class-bound nature of the system; second, and perhaps more importantly, by working on this economic base it can transform the relationship between the economic and cultural spheres and thus change the balance of influence between them.

The school therefore can be one site of struggle, and Apple indicates the different elements that contribute to the reproduction of the system but also allow the possibility of struggle and transformation.

> It became clear that at least three basic elements in schooling had to be examined. These included: the day to day interactions and regularities of the hidden curriculum that tacitly taught important norms and values; the formal corpus of school knowledge – that is, the overt curriculum itself – that is planned and found in the various materials and texts and filtered through teachers; and finally, the fundamental perspectives that educators (read here Gramsci's point about the role of intellectuals) use to plan, organize, and evaluate what happens in schools.
>
> (Apple, 1995, pp. 20–1)

In relation to schools, then, there are three specific sites of resistance: the informal and hidden aspects of the curriculum, the formal curriculum itself, and the values and belief systems of teachers.

Symbolic control

Apple (1995; 2000) has written about the power of texts in a number of places. Curriculum texts used in schools constitute one way by which the state has gradually increased its authority over the field of symbolic control. His contention is that this control is designed to change 'the very consciousness of society' (Apple, 1995, p. 56) and, using a phrase coined by Basil Bernstein (1985), he designates the state as a recontextualising agency. I have already made the point that pedagogic knowledge is different from knowledge as it was originally conceived, and that knowledge undergoes a process of transformation as it is used in the classroom. This constitutes an internal transformatory process.

Apple, in contrast, has focused on external processes of transformation so that knowledge is made official in part through the recontextualising apparatus of the state. In the United Kingdom, this process has been formally codified in a national curriculum. In the United States of America, the external recontextualising process has involved a series of complicated political manoeuvres, and Apple (1988) provides one example of this in his history of textbook production and influence. Official knowledge is compromised knowledge and never a pure act of domination on behalf of powerful interest groups at the expense of less powerful ones.

The 'cultural capital' declared to be official knowledge, then, is *compromised* knowledge, knowledge that is filtered through a complicated set of political screens and decisions before it gets to be declared official knowledge. This affects what knowledge is selected and what the selected knowledge looks like as it is transformed into something that will be taught to students in school. In this way, the State acts as what Basil Bernstein would call a 'recontextualising agent' in the process of symbolic control as it creates accords that enable the creation of 'knowledge for everyone'.

(Apple, 1996, p. 57)

These political accords shape the way knowledge is organised at the classroom level. They do this in three ways. The first of these is that the knowledge and the form that it takes is fundamentally different from how it was originally conceived by researchers, for example, or by oppressed groups. What happens is that the text's external relations or its inter-text changes, so that it is positioned differently with regard to other texts and other educational practices. This has the effect, as Apple reminds us, of altering power relations. Second, the power of the state, though not complete, has given the educational text greater power than it ever had as an unrecontextualised text. This works not just through the imposition of sanctions (coercive power) but also through productive forms of power, so that the acceptable discourse in terms of what can be thought and acted upon by teachers and students is now structured differently. For Apple, it is now structured around 'a different set of political and cultural needs and principles' (Apple, 1995, p. 57).

Finally, pedagogical knowledge at the classroom level also impacts on these recontextualising agencies such as the publishing industry, so that knowledge is shaped in a particular way that is politically acceptable and at the same time is simplified so that it can be easily assessed. This recontextualising process reorganises and shapes knowledge differently so that education and the curriculum now have a different purpose, for example better to meet the demands of an economic perspective or to fit with the dictates of a neoconservative traditional agenda. Apple therefore has a clear normative agenda, though at times in his writing he makes sympathetic noises towards postmodernism. For example, in his book *Official Knowledge, Democratic Education in a Conservative Age* (2000), he focuses on the construction of textbook knowledge, and he is concerned to develop a theory about how these textbooks are used and read. For him, texts allow multiple interpretations, though there are always preferred readings. Furthermore these preferred readings are supported by institutional and pedagogic arrangements which allow some messages to have greater influence than others.

He parts company with post-modernist thought in his explicit desire to develop this ethical agenda. It is hardly a surprise to work out what this is:

When thoughtful educators remind us that curriculum and teaching always end in an act of personal knowledge, they also tacitly remind us

> that no matter how grounded our critical investigations are (and *must be*) in an equally critical understanding of the larger relations of dominance and subordination of this society and in the micropolitics of our institutions, it ultimately comes down to a recognition that we, as persons, participate in these relations. We have a responsibility to say 'no' to as many of them that are antidemocratic as we can and to act to affirm what is less dominative and more caring.
>
> (Apple, 2000, p. 13)

This also points to the need for educators to adopt a reflexive stance, an important theme of Apple's work.

There are two principal problems with this position. The first refers to the way knowledge is constructed by individual students sitting in real classrooms whose real-life concerns may be outside schools and outside the environments in which the official knowledge is being reproduced. The second would seem to follow from this. The constituency he speaks for is not necessarily a progressive or united one. Oppressed people, with notable exceptions, tend to behave in ways of which liberally minded academics such as Michael Apple would disapprove. Removing structural inequalities and reshaping curriculum and pedagogic paths so that those who have hitherto been dispossessed of a voice are given one may lead to a situation which is less democratic and more autocratic than that which it replaced. Apple, however, is determined to show that curriculum-making is not a natural or essentialist activity, but a constructed one; and, furthermore, constructed in conditions in which there are more powerful and less powerful voices. Official curricula therefore have significant effects on the way society makes and remakes itself.

> It has been argued in considerable detail elsewhere that the selection and organisation of knowledge in schools is an ideological process, one that serves the interests of particular classes and social groups. However . . . this does not mean that the entire corpus of school knowledge is a mirror reflection of ruling class ideas, imposed in an unmediated and coercive manner. Instead, the processes of cultural incorporation are dynamic, reflecting both continuities and contradictions of that dominant culture and the continual remaking and relegitimation of that culture's plausibility system.
>
> (Apple, 2000, pp. 55–6)

His documentation of the struggles over the curriculum allows him to develop a non-statist view of the policy process.

> Yet the powerful are not that powerful. The politics of official knowledge are the politics of accords or compromises. They are usually not

impositions, but signify how dominant groups try to create situations where the compromises that are formed favour them.

(Apple, 2000, p. 10)

Though he makes much of the various recontextualising processes which knowledge undergoes before it becomes official pedagogic knowledge, he is always careful to indicate the limitations of the state, and he does not see the process by which this official knowledge is constructed as a simplistic one of powerful people deciding what less powerful people should know and learn. As he argues, the hegemony of the state, and elites which dominate its workings, is always 'fragile, always temporary and is constantly subject to threat. There will always be openings for counter-hegemonic activity' (Apple, 2000, p. 10). He is careful, though, not to romanticise, and in the process make exaggerated claims about what can be achieved by dispossessed and relatively powerless groups. As he argues, the conservative restoration round the world has been extremely powerful and effective, and perhaps points once again to the inability of the left to mobilise itself in defence of principles of equity and social justice.

Basil Bernstein (1996) examined a different but related aspect of curriculum provision, that of the differential access which different fractions of the school population have to the curriculum. However, his concern is not specifically with the contents of the curriculum per se, but with the pedagogical process and the way this constructs knowledge and identity for different sets of students. A further concern is with teacher identities and in relation to this he identified three broad categories. The retrospective pedagogic identity has as its reference point narratives of the past, to which current models of practice are compared. It advocates a strongly classified and strongly framed curriculum for schools. The second teacher identity that Bernstein suggests is prospective, looks towards the future and is essentially concerned with ensuring the efficient performance of the economy. It pays due deference to traditional forms of the curriculum and, though less concerned with strong classification, advocates argue for strong framing by teachers. The third model proposed by Bernstein is a decentred identity, either instrumental or therapeutic. The instrumental variety is market-orientated and locally embedded. The therapeutic version locates teachers in principled discourses about the purposes of education and is inclusive. The next chapter then examines Bernstein's theories of education as they relate to the curriculum.

Chapter 7

Basil Bernstein on pedagogy

Basil Bernstein wrote extensively on a number of related issues, but principally his work focused on three key areas: language and social class, the construction of the curriculum, and knowledge development. For Bernstein, sociologists of education foregrounded the contents of the curriculum and attempted to build theories which explain how power relations are relayed externally through the formal mechanisms of education: for example, how social class relations persist across generations. In contrast, his major concern has been the internal or intrinsic features of pedagogic discourse that structure the content of the curriculum and how it is differentially distributed between different social groups. Knowledge or indeed different types of knowledge are therefore not relayed in an unmediated fashion from the external world to the internal environment of the school and thence to the pupils, but are recontextualised in terms of the way pupils pedagogically access them. The focus is therefore on the pedagogic device, rather than the contents of the curriculum per se; and this pedagogic device works according to distribution, recontextualisation and evaluation rules. These rules are constructed in terms of the strength of the boundaries between different organising ideas. As Diaz (2001, pp. 84–5) argues:

> there is a close relation in Bernstein between boundaries, power, social groups, and forms of identity. Bernstein's analysis of power and boundaries provokes questions about their force, duration of spacing, ordering of internal forms and sites for knowledge, flows of identity, and relations with changes in the collective basis of society.

These boundaries refer to both knowledge and contexts. In terms of the latter, it is possible to see how recognition rules operating within school settings serve to advantage some children at the expense of others, not, it should be noted, because those children who are disadvantaged are unable to use the different modes of thought, but because recognition and realisation rules are differentially distributed.

Moore (2005, p. 140), for example, suggests the following:

> What are differentially distributed between groups are the recognition
> and realisation rules and orientations to meaning whereby they can
> successfully distinguish between that which can be assumed and taken for
> granted and that which is calling for a demonstration of understanding
> within a specific context such as a classroom, tutorial or examination.
> These issues of recognition and realisation become problematic for many
> children when the ideology of the pedagogy (as with progressivism) denies
> that such demands are being made, as if the child is free to be the 'author'
> of the text.

It is their understanding of, and ability to respond in an appropriate manner
to, these recognition and realisation rules which structure the pedagogic
regime within formal schooling, and not their ability to respond in appropriate
ways to the contents of the curriculum.

These recognition and realisation rules, then, are crucial to the success or
otherwise of various strata of children within schooling, and mark the way
power operates to maintain boundaries between different fractions of the
school population, and consequently structures relations within society. As
Bernstein notes, contexts have different properties and the relations between
these different contexts can be codified in terms of a number of key concepts.
Classification is one such concept, as Bernstein, looking back on previous
work, makes clear:

> I started with classification because classification, strong or weak, marks
> the distinguishing features of a context. For example, some children when
> they first go to school are unaware or unsure of what is expected of them.
> They fail to recognise the distinguishing features which provide the
> school/classroom with its unique features and so particular identity. Such
> a failure in recognition will necessarily lead to inappropriate behaviour.
> On the other hand, some children are extensively prepared and are aware
> of the difference between the family context and the school context. In this
> case they are able to recognise the distinguishing features of the school, or
> class, even if they are not always able to produce the range of behaviour
> the school expects. Inasmuch as some children recognise the distin-
> guishing features of the school, relative to the children who do not, those
> that do are in a more powerful position with respect to the school. It is
> likely that those who do recognise the distinguishing features of the school
> are more likely to be middle class children than lower working class
> children. The basis of such recognition is a strong classification between
> the context of the family and the context of the school. In our example the
> strong classification between the family and the school is a product of

the symbolic power of the middle class family. This power is translated
into the child's power of recognition with its advantageous outcomes.
... We can therefore set up a relationship between the principles of
classification and the recognition rules for identifying the specificity or the
similarity of contexts. As the classification principle is established by
power relations and the relays of power relations, then recognition rules
confer power relative to those who lack them.

(Bernstein, 2000, pp. 104–5, quoted in Moore, 2005, p. 138)

Though Bernstein was extensively criticised for the deficit nature of his
theory – certain fractions of the working class do not have the capacity to access
the rules which underpin formal schooling – he consistently denied that this
was his intention. His purpose was to understand how children's embeddedness in specific contexts has meant that their responses, or at least the way they
access recognition and realisation rules within formal settings, serves to
disadvantage some at the expense of others.

Language and social class

It is the relations between language and social class that we need to address
first. This is the most widely known part of his work and formed the principal
part of his thinking in the first period of his career. In typical Bernsteinian
fashion he developed a series of codes to explain the relation between language
use and school relations. Though his work on language codes underwent some
modification, not least in the terminology he used, he settled eventually on
describing two language codes: a restricted or public code and an elaborated
or private code. These codes differ from each other in a number of distinctive
ways.

A restricted code is particularistic, context-free and implicit, whereas
an extended code is universalistic, context-free and explicit. These are the
principal differences between the two types of code, though Bernstein does
suggest other ways by which they can be distinguished, but these are less
important. The first of these, the particularistic/universalistic dichotomy,
relates to the way language is used to refer in the first instance to a local set of
circumstances, and in the second instance to a wider or more universal set
of circumstances. Bernstein illustrates these with reference to a classification
experiment that was performed whereby the child using a particularistic form
of language, when asked to relate together types of food, replied that these
were the types of food that they ate at breakfast or that were cooked at home.
The child who responded in a universalistic way described them as vegetables
or seafood. In the first case reference is made to a particular and familiar
setting; in the second to the formal and universalistic way they are defined,
without reference to the particular setting that is familiar to the child. It is
important here not to suggest that one form of code is a more correct way

of classifying than the other, only that reference is made to different ways of classifying.

There is no suggestion in Bernstein's work that ways of classifying and contextualising objects in the world can be arranged in a hierarchical fashion; he only observes as an empirical fact that there exist different ways to classify objects in the world. In a previous chapter the issue of classifying events and experiences in the world was examined, and the argument was made that particular systems of classification do not have a transcendental quality but are conventions generated through countless decisions made by groups of people living in societies. However, within the context discussed here, the point is that two groups of children with different backgrounds and family experiences chose to classify common and familiar objects in different types of ways. The second point to be made about classifications is that regardless of their correctness or not, they have powerful effects; and thus if the different ways of classifying can be shown to apply to different types of children, and further that the schools to which these children go can also be shown to operate through systems that favour one type of classifying scheme over another, then a possible explanation for the relative social disadvantage of one group over another is provided. However, with regard to this experiment Bernstein is careful to argue that when asked to reclassify, the children who in the first instance chose to operate with a particularistic code were then able to switch to a universalistic code and vice versa. It was therefore not the capability of the children that was the determining factor in their choices, but their immediate concerns and preoccupations. In other words, the answer they gave was the one that they considered to be most appropriate in the circumstances.

The two other dichotomies, context-bound/context-free and implicit/explicit, can be explained as sub-sets of the first dichotomy. The first of these is where the specific context of the action is the referential point for the speaker, rather than in the more elaborated code, where specific context is reduced and the language used refers to or could refer to a wider range of contexts, which are frequently implicit. The second of these is where the description of an action makes some assumptions about the context of the story which they are telling – assuming these to be understood and therefore not in need of an explicit rendition. They are literally implicit. Bernstein's point is that in school, children are required to use a language code which is universalistic, context-free and explicit. Again, it is not that some children do not have a capacity to use such a language, it is that when a task is set for them in school, they understand the task as being one in which a restricted code is sufficient, and this is clearly in conflict with what is expected in school. He argues this point in the following way:

> It is not that the working-class children do not have in their passive vocabulary the vocabulary used by the middle-class children. Nor is it the case that the children differ in their tacit understanding of the

linguistic rule system. Rather, what we have here are differences in the use of language arising out of a specific context.

(Bernstein, 1975, p. 179)

As a result of choosing to adopt different codes, the two sets of children use language in different ways. So, for example, a restricted code-user is inclined to use more catchphrases, with the implicit understanding that meaning is shared, and more pronouns; an elaborated speaker will introduce longer pauses between phrases and use fewer pronouns. Indeed, these logically follow from the characteristics that have been used to define the two types of language codes.

We now come to the identification of the two types of code-users. For Bernstein, these two codes corresponded to fractions of working- and middle-class children. Indeed, his theory of linguistic codes was underpinned by a theory of class. Furthermore, since his work was empirically based, the identification of these class fractions was not dependent on their propensity to use elaborated or restricted codes. Such identification was a result of other work-related and positional factors, and Bernstein's theory seeks to explain why one set of children was relatively successful at school, whereas the other was less so. Class, and the consequent placing of children, persons and families in class categories, is perhaps a more fluid concept than it once was. For example, Ball (2003, p. 11) writes that:

> As should already be apparent my discussion of class here does not rest primarily upon any 'independently defined structure of positions' (Parkin, 1979, p. 113) but rather collective modes of social action and social practices are taken as the defining features of class.

And thus self-attribution is considered at least by Ball to be an essential element in such categorisation. However, what Bernstein is seeking to do is identify an example of a social practice which is not shared by all children in formal education.

Classification and framing

The second principal theme of Bernstein's work, closely related to the first, was the relations between different items of knowledge. The two most important types of relations are: the degree of integration between different knowledge domains; and progression within the domain itself. The first of these is the degree of knowledge integration. A curriculum may be understood as strongly or weakly classified and as strongly or weakly framed. A strongly classified curriculum is defined by Bernstein (1990) as having clearly delineated domains of knowledge with strong boundaries between them; conversely, a weakly classified curriculum is understood as having weak boundaries between the different knowledge domains. A strongly framed curriculum, on the other hand, is defined as a programme of study in which teacher and student have limited control over the selection of items and the way it is organised in respect of the pedagogical relationship. A weakly framed curriculum is characterised by greater control by teacher and student over the selection of content, the way it is organised and its pacing. Bernstein, in relation to the first of these principles, classification, identifies two types of curricula: 'collection codes' where strong boundaries between domains are present, and 'integrated codes' where weak boundaries are in evidence.

Fogarty (1991) has identified ten models of curriculum integration and these range from strongly classified and strongly framed curricula, as in the traditional approach, to weakly classified and weakly framed or networked approaches to curriculum planning. Between the two extremes – traditional and networked approaches – she identifies eight other points on the continuum: connected, nested, sequenced, shared, webbed, threaded, integrated and immersed. Fogarty (1991) then provides in her book *The Mindful School: How to Integrate the Curriculum* more detail about these different approaches:

1   A *fragmented curriculum*: here there are clear boundaries between the different subjects and thus this first type cannot reasonably be thought of as integrated in any sense. Subject delineations are clear-cut, they are taught in separate blocks on the timetable, they have their own formal knowledge structure, and content is treated as distinctive and belonging to the specific area.

2   A *connected curriculum*: reference is made to other content areas, connections are sought and suggestions are made as to how knowledge in another domain can supplement and contribute to knowledge in the specified domain.

3   A *nested curriculum*: a distinction is made between generic skills and specific content. This form is only partially integrated as the content of the subject area is still treated as specific to a curriculum area; however, some common skills are identified which cross the boundaries between different content areas and these are taught across the curriculum.

4   A *sequenced curriculum*: here deliberately planned topics are arranged to be taught at the same time so that children moving between different subject areas are taught the same concept albeit that reference is made to a different application and a different discipline in two or more different contexts. For example, statistical probability is taught in mathematics and in social science to reinforce the learning of the concept and to allow students to understand how it can be used in different contexts.

5   A *shared curriculum*: a particular topic is chosen which has a number of different disciplinary strands. Teachers from different subject disciplines are partnered and teach different aspects of the topic.

6 A *webbed curriculum*: this is very much like a shared curriculum, the difference being that there is a greater degree of integration. The curriculum is divided into themes and each theme is treated in a different way by different subject teachers. Thus the integrity of each discipline is retained, and the methods and approaches that are distinctive to these disciplines are taught even if the generic subject matter is the same.

7 A *threaded curriculum*: the emphasis is on the process of learning, or on what might be called a meta-theoretical process. The content is subordinated to the teaching of these skills and a curriculum is devised which cuts across the traditional disciplines and focuses on common skills. In this scenario, the traditional and highly classified curriculum is abandoned for a new set of delineations and boundaries, based round different types of skill. Clearly within each discipline in the traditional curriculum skills were featured; these skills, however, were content-specific. A threaded curriculum offers a weakly classified curriculum in that skills and content are treated as separate.

8 An *integrated curriculum*: here disciplinary boundaries begin to dissolve, as teachers work in inter-disciplinary teams to plan units round overlapping concepts and themes.

9 An *immersed curriculum*: integration becomes the responsibility of the learner as they focus on a particular topic or theme, and they borrow ideas, theories, skills and the like from different disciplines. There is little evidence here of any adherence to the methods and protocols embedded within particular disciplines. The disciplines themselves are treated as impediments to the development of knowledge and this strong classification is transgressively dissolved.

10 A *networked approach to curriculum planning*: Kysilka (1998, p. 199) suggests that such an approach 'requires learners to reorganise relationships of ideas within and between the separate disciplines as well as ideas and learning strategies within and between learners'.

Each of these forms of integration can be positioned along a continuum, with a fragmented curriculum in Bernstein's terms being strongly classified and framed, in contrast to networking approaches to curriculum planning which are weakly classified and weakly framed.

However, for Bernstein, such typologies were never enough; indeed, he sought to distance himself from the notion of an ideal type. His concern was always with power distributions in society, identity formation as a result of these power distributions and how social control was exercised: 'How a society selects, classifies, distributes, transmits and evaluates the educational knowledge it considers to be public, reflects both the distribution of power and the principles of social control' (Bernstein, 1971, p. 47).

Three message systems, curriculum, pedagogy and evaluation, are implicated in these principles of social control: 'Curriculum defines what counts as valid knowledge, pedagogy defines what counts as the valid transmission of knowledge, and evaluation defines what counts as a valid realisation of knowledge' (Bernstein, 1971, p. 48). In relation to the curriculum, Bernstein is referring to the boundary between various contents that delineate one form of knowledge from another. If there is a strong degree of insulation between them, then Bernstein is inclined to describe the resulting curriculum as closed. If there is a weak degree of insulation, then the curriculum can be defined as open. Further to this a curriculum which exhibits a strong degree of insulation can be called a collection type, whereas a curriculum which displays the opposite features can be called an integrated type.

For Bernstein, what distinguishes a collection from an integrated type of curriculum is the strength of the boundaries between the contents. Classification and framing provide the means by which these can be understood. Bernstein is here referring to the relationship between contents and not the contents themselves. Strong classification then refers to a curriculum in which the various parts are strongly insulated from each other. Weak classification refers to a curriculum where there is weak insulation between the various parts. Furthermore, classification refers to the structure of one of the message systems, the curriculum. A second message system, pedagogy, is to be understood in terms of framing and again this should be understood not in terms of the content of the pedagogy in use but the degree of insulation between the different forms; in the case of pedagogy, it refers to the relationship between the teacher and the learner. Thus Bernstein provides us with a clear definition of framing. It 'refers to the degree of control teacher and pupil possess over the selection, organisation and pacing of the knowledge transmitted and received in the pedagogical relationship' (Bernstein, 1971, p. 51).

In addition, there is a further relationship which Bernstein wishes to bring to our attention. This is the relationship between everyday knowledge and the knowledge which is transmitted in school as part of the pedagogical exchange. Again, this can be understood as either strongly or weakly framed, depending on the degree of insulation between the two contents. The various strengths of the code in relation to classification and framing may vary independently of each other, so a curriculum may be strongly classified, yet weakly framed; or it may be weakly classified and strongly framed. Furthermore, framing, being defined in terms of selection, organisation and pacing, may vary between these three sub-elements. Thus pedagogy may be strongly organised but weakly paced. However, the identification of these pedagogic forms can be misleading. A type of pedagogy which on the surface allows considerable licence for the pupil in the development of the knowledge subset may in reality be strongly framed, because the teacher is highly skilled in eliciting answers from her pupils that are commensurate with what was intended in the first place. The pupil is being led to certain conclusions even though on the surface this would not be constituted as a transmission form of pedagogy.

Classification is an easier form to understand since it refers to the boundaries between classes of curriculum content. Two points need to be made about it. First, it produces a subject loyalty amongst teachers and thus strong boundaries between subjects are likely to be maintained at the school because previous socialisation into the subject discipline has already occurred: 'Any attempt to weaken or change the classification strength may be felt as a threat to one's identity and may be experienced as a pollution endangering the sacred' (Bernstein, 1971, p. 59). The second point is that the formation of these specific identities, resulting in a desire to maintain strong boundaries between subjects, is likely to be reflected in control over the type of framing that is instituted; and indeed, the relationship between classification and framing is the key to understanding the different types of curriculum forms that exist.

It is here that Bernstein's definition of framing is misleading, notwithstanding his note that the various parts of the framing device can vary independently of each other. Attaching the strength of a frame to the control that teachers and pupils can exert over the selection, organisation and pacing of knowledge creates a tendency to view framing as extending to teachers and pupils operating in conjunction with each other. There may be a situation where the pedagogic relation between teachers and pupils is such that framing constitutes a disjunction between them.

Knowledge systems

The third area of concern for Bernstein (1996) relates to the way knowledge is constructed. He developed a set of categories to delineate different types of symbolic systems. He distinguished between horizontal and vertical forms of discourse, and then added a further distinction within the latter between hierarchical and horizontal knowledge forms. Horizontal forms of discourse are described by Bernstein (1996, pp. 170–1) as: 'the form of knowledge usually typified as everyday, oral or common-sense knowledge [which] has a group of features: local, segmental, context dependent, tacit, multi-layered, often contradictory across contexts but not within contexts'.

Vertical discourses, by contrast, are defined in terms of two characteristics: verticality and grammaticality. Verticality denotes the way theory is developed and it can take two forms. The first of these is hierarchical where the constructs that form the mode of knowledge can be arranged in a hierarchical fashion, starting at the base of the pyramidal structure with more concrete propositions and moving upwards to more general and abstract principles which are effectively integrated within a hierarchical structure. However, some knowledge bases have a horizontal structure which consists of the proliferation of more and more specialised forms or languages which are incommensurable with each other. An example of this might be the field of education. For Bernstein, this weak horizontal structure has certain consequences, principally that

every new approach becomes a social movement or sect which immediately defines the nature of the subject by re-defining what is to be
admitted, and what is beyond the pale, so that with every new approach
the subject almost starts from scratch.

(Bernstein, 1977, p. 167)

Whereas this type of knowledge form is concerned with internality – the
relations between the parts of the discourse that are internal to itself – Bernstein
develops a further relation which attempts to connect it to the empirical world
– grammaticality. Some knowledge bases then have a weak capacity to 'generate
empirical correlates' (Moore and Muller, 2002) and therefore a weak capacity
to progress as a form of knowledge; whereas others have a strong relationship
with the empirical world, have developed a strong language for confirming or
disconfirming theory, and therefore have a greater capacity for progression.

This approach by Bernstein is very different from that adopted by Hirst
and the foundationalists. For them, the issue of curriculum is dominated
by the question of knowledge. Children's differential ability to access that
knowledge can be explained either by the different capacities those different
children have (innate abilities); or by the different curricula different types
of children are exposed to (structural arrangements); or by the different personal
dispositions that they have acquired (i.e. immediate as opposed to deferred
gratification traits). For Bernstein, the issue of differential access to the
curriculum lies with the different abilities and inclinations those children
have to recognise and realise the rules that constitute the pedagogic discourse
they are confronted with in schools.

The issue that we are then immediately confronted with is the status and
constitution of those rules. If Bernstein is merely sketching out a meta-theory
to contextualise the specific rules found in specific schools, and these specific
rules are differently constituted in different schools, both actual and possible
ones, then the same relativist and contextualised description applies to both
the specific realisation of those rules and to the general theoretical framework
developed by Bernstein.

It is also important not to lose sight of the degree to which the contents of
the curriculum and type of knowledge that underpins it actually shape the
specific realisation and recognition rules in operation in specific settings. As
Stenhouse has suggested, pedagogic forms which stress inquiry-based modes
of realisation are underpinned by a different conception of knowledge, what it
consists of and how it can be used, from knowledge which is better expressed
through didactic modes of realisation. A further influence on the advocacy of
what Bernstein has called an integrated code was the early work of the Russian
psychologist Lev Vygotsky and in particular his locating of learning in the
social sphere.

Chapter 8

Lev Vygotsky and internalisation

Bernstein foregrounded the pedagogical relationship as the key to understanding how different class fractions of children were able to access the curriculum in schools. Lev Vygotsky, writing in the early part of the twentieth century, proposed a view of learning which is in opposition to didactic modes of pedagogy and rote learning procedures, and this radical approach was to have a profound effect on subsequent ways of understanding teaching and learning. Deep learning, for Vygotsky, has a number of features. It is an active meaning-making process for the child, involves progression in the thinking capacity of the child so that he or she learns in a different way from an adult and understands everyday concepts as being qualitatively different from scientific concepts, and it cannot be effectively delivered through didactic and rote learning methods.

Internalisation and participation

In psychology, with specific reference to pedagogy, two models of learning have been identified, and these can serve as oppositional ends on a continuum with a number of other positions taken between them. Daniels (2001) describes these two models as an internalisation thesis and a participation antithesis, and both offer a different perspective on the relation between the individual or the psychological and the social or the collective. Matusov (1998, p. 326, quoted in Daniels, 2001, p. 39) describes the difference in the two approaches:

> The internalisation model of cultural development, emphasising transformation of social functions into individual skills, leads to a chain of mutually related dualisms between oppositional abstractions such as the social and the individual, the external and the internal, and the environment and the organism. Attempts to bridge these dualistic gaps seem problematic because these dual abstractions mutually constitute each other and are, thus, inseparable from the beginning. . . . The participation model considers individual cultural development as a validated process of transformation of individual participation in sociocultural activity.

Transformation of participation involves assuming changed responsibility for the activity, redefining membership in a community of practice, and changing the sociocultural practice itself.

With the internalisation model, the individual is treated as entirely separate from the environment in which they operate. There is a time lag between the messages received by the individual which have originated in society and their reception, assimilation and transformation by each individual.

The participation model, taken up by Lave and Wenger (1991) and Wenger (1998), recognises a more active role for the individual, and learners enter into external worlds as they learn; indeed, the dualisms inherent in inner/outer worlds, and psychological/social domains are blurred.

> The concept of 'flower' is not actually more general than the concept of 'rose'. When the child has mastered only a single concept, its relationship to the object is different than it is after he [*sic*] masters a second. However, after he masters a second concept, there is a long period during which the concept of 'flower' continues to stand alongside, rather than above, the concept of 'rose'. The former does not include the latter. The narrower concept is not subordinated. Rather, the broader concept acts as a substitute for the narrower one. It stands alongside it in a single series. When the concept 'flower' is generalised, the relationship between it and the concept of 'rose' changes as well. Indeed, there is a change in its relationship with all subordinate concepts. This marks the emergence of a concept system.
>
> (Vygotsky, 1987, p. 193)

This has implications for the effectiveness of certain types of instruction or pedagogy, since didactic approaches, for Vygotsky, lead to an empty form of learning.

> Pedagogical experience demonstrates that direct instruction in concepts is impossible. It is pedagogically fruitless. The teacher who attempts to use this approach achieves nothing but a mindless learning of words, an empty verbalism that stimulates or imitates the presence of concepts in the child. Under these conditions, the child learns not the concept but the word, and this word is taken over by the child through memory rather than thought. Such knowledge turns out to be inadequate in any meaningful application. This mode of instruction is the basic defect of the purely scholastic verbal mode of teaching which has been universally condemned. It substitutes the learning of dead empty verbal schemes for the mastery of living knowledge.
>
> (Vygotsky, 1987, p. 170)

The mastery of living knowledge implies that concepts have to be internalised, reconstituted within frameworks that the leaner already holds and then made usable. Matusov (1998) suggests some clear distinctions between internalisation and participation, and he also makes the point that Vygotsky's thinking never moved very far along the continuum between the two. Matusov identifies these differences in the following way. Internalisation separates the social and psychological planes of being, with the social dimension of learning preceding in time the psychological. Individual activity in learning is therefore distinct from collective activity, and this suggests that individual activity is always more advanced than collective activity. As a result, a notion of transfer between the collective and the individual is needed. The course of learning development in the child is therefore set by human nature, has an end-point to which it works, and can be objectively defined.

At the other end of the continuum is the participation antithesis, where the psychological and social planes mutually constitute each other, and each in turn contributes to the evolution of the other. 'Solo activities occur in the context of socio-cultural activity rather than as context free mental functions' (Daniels, 2001: 40). The notion of transfer is dispensed with, as meaning-making by the learner is a process of continual reinterpretation and, more fundamentally, renegotiation. Finally, it is the learner who is central to their process of development, and has an active and intentional part to play in the direction of their learning trajectory.

Vygotsky has been interpreted in a number of different ways and it would be false to suggest that his work should be interpreted as an internalisation thesis without reference to those features which Matusov suggested comprise the participation antithesis. For example, Vygotsky moved from his early insistence that the course of development has a set and universal pattern to it, to a position where he accepted that these trajectories have an undeniably social and therefore relativistic element to them. These debates about learning are echoed in current debates about computational and socio-cultural approaches, and have implications for the types of pedagogy that can and should be adopted and for the types of knowledge that should underpin the curriculum. Vygotsky's most significant contribution to learning theory rests with his identification of a zone of proximal development, which relates not only to pedagogy and curriculum, but more significantly to assessment and evaluation as well.

Zone of proximal development

For Vygotsky, decontextualised forms of assessment, separated out from the teaching and learning process, cannot deliver what is intended:

> Suppose I investigate two children upon entrance into school, both of whom are twelve years old chronologically and eight years old in terms of mental development. Can I say that they are the same age mentally? Of

course. What does this mean? It means that they can independently deal with tasks up to the degree of difficulty that has been standardised for the eight-year-old. If I stop at this point, people would imagine that the subsequent course of development and of school learning of these children will be the same, because it depends on their intellect. . . . Now imagine that I do not terminate my study at this point, but only begin it. . . . Suppose I show . . . [these children] have various ways of dealing with a task . . . that the children solve the problem with my assistance. Under these circumstances it turns out that the first child can deal with problems up to a twelve-year-old's level. The second up to a nine-year-old's. Now are these children mentally the same? When it was first shown that the capability of children with equal levels of mental development to learn under a teacher's guidance varied to a high degree, it became apparent that those children were not mentally the same and the subsequent course of their learning would obviously be different. This difference between twelve and eight, or between nine and eight, is what is called the zone of proximal development.

(Vygotsky, 1978, pp. 85–6)

Four general versions of the zone of proximal development have been formulated. Whether they are applications, extensions or reconstructions of Vygotskian intentions is outside the scope of this chapter, concerned as it is with the relationship of his conceptual apparatus to the study of the curriculum. Daniels (2001) describes these as assessment, scaffolding, cultural and collectivist versions.

The assessment version focuses on a new and radical way of understanding how we should assess the capability of the child. Broadly, this view is counter-poised to two other views of assessment: performance and competence. In the performance mode, what is being assessed is the performance of the child in relation to other children taking the test, and in formal schooling these children are usually of the same age. This entails a form of standardisation, both of the test conditions and of the way it is marked, thus the emphasis is on a child's performance in strictly controlled conditions which are applied to all the children taking the text. The context of the performance is therefore crucial to how the child performs. This is compared with the second view of assessment where instead of the child being assessed in terms of their performance in a highly regulated setting, it is the competence of the child at that moment in time which is the focus of the assessment. In other words, the child is understood as having a number of dispositions, and an amount of knowledge which is now the focus of the assessment, and its determination has to be separated from the formal context of performance, such as in an examination. The difference between the two constructs can be expressed conceptually as above, but also in terms of the different results for each child from the assessments.

Table 1 Error types in relating performance to competence

	Success on task	*Failure on task*
Child has underlying competence (to a sufficient degree)	Performance correlated with competence	False negative error: failure due to factor other than lack of competence
Child does not have underlying competence (to a sufficient degree)	False positive error: success due to factor other than competence	Performance correlated with competence

Source: Wood and Power (1987).

Wood and Power (1987) distinguish between performance and competence (see Table 1) and develop this distinction along two axes. The first relates to performance in the test situation – whether the child is successful or unsuccessful at the task. The second axis refers to what the child can do. Thus two types of error may result – false negative and false positive – and these occur because of the gap between competence and performance.

Though this syllogism is immediately attractive, it has within it a number of problems. It is difficult to distinguish performance from competence in any meaningful way because the performance achieved by the child influences what and how they learn and therefore affects the competence levels achieved by that child at a later point in time. Indeed, the type of knowledge that is absorbed through a formal process of instruction is determined by the type of assessment that the child will subsequently undergo. Second, the gap between competence and performance varies and cannot be measured in any straightforward way, since for some children it is those factors which inhere in the testing process itself which sustain the gap between performance and competence. This gap cannot be measured because the measuring of it is subject to the same type of inaccuracy. The point, however, is that both competence and performance are understood as the child performing unaided during the assessment process. Vygotsky's version of the assessment process is radical in that it focuses on the development of the child and thus on his or her capability under the guidance of an expert. It has a closer connection with what the child will be able to do unaided, not currently but in the future. It is developmental in origin, and involves a reconceptualisation of the notion of assessment, because it ties together instruction and assessment. Finally, it cannot be standardised, because the type and degree of support given to the child which is now an essential part of the assessment process differs and should differ in relation to the needs of the child. However, this is one version, as I suggested above, of the zone of proximal development.

The second and more contentious version comprises scaffolding. The expert or scaffolder constructs, in relation to their understanding of the needs of the child, a scaffold or pathway to the acquiring of knowledge by the child, and presents it to the child. The child then follows the implicit and explicit rules of the scaffolding and acquires the new knowledge. There is no negotiation involved in the development of the scaffold with the child. Diagnosis of the child's needs and state of readiness is undertaken by the other or expert; they then construct a learning programme based on this initial diagnosis and support the child through this learning programme. This can be compared with a different form of scaffolding, where the child not only undertakes a programme of learning in relation to their zone of proximal development, but is involved in the development of this programme. Moll (1990) suggests that Vygotsky was ambivalent about the specific form the scaffolding should take, and merely described elements of that scaffolding without specifying the precise role the child would play in its development. These elements include demonstration, asking leading questions and introducing the initial elements of the task's solution. Whether the form of the scaffolding was negotiated with the child or not was left unanswered, since these three elements could form a part of either an imposed or a negotiated settlement with a child.

Clearly, this model of scaffolding is dependent on the idea of the expert also being the facilitator; and it is hard to see within the constraints of this model what the role of the expert would be unless the programme of work was in some sense constructed and delivered by someone with a greater knowledge of the process of learning. The child is unlikely, given their developmental state, to be able to construct such a programme; because if they could then there would be no need for a relationship with an expert. In so far as this suggest an either/or picture of the process, it is misleading. There are a number of in-between situations in which elements of negotiation are present. These might include: the desirability of involving the child in the diagnostic process because only they have sufficient knowledge of their learning needs; or the positioning of the child so that they take a full, engaged and willing part in the scaffolding process for it to work. These two in-between positions reflect different views on the nature of the negotiated process that comprises scaffolding.

Scaffolding, then, is a form of guidance in which the novice engages with the expert to solve a problem or carry out a task. The zone of proximal development refers to the gap between the novice and the expert and scaffolding is used as a way of bridging this gap. Clearly, the novice is incapable of bridging this gap alone and thus the active intervention of the expert is necessary to allow it to happen. In this sense of scaffolding, the expert is understood as a pedagogic expert though they will also have expert knowledge of the process that the initiate is being inducted into. Bruner (1996), for example, using a Vygotskian meta-theory, argues that the internalisation of culture requires a particular set of pedagogic principles which underpin the exchange: a concordance between what a learner can do and what the cultural message which is being transmitted offers; an expert who can intuit what the learner needs and who then devises appropriate ways of delivering it; and a shared agreement between expert and learner about how such 'an intersubjective arrangement is supposed to work canonically *in this particular culture*' (Bruner, 1996, p. 69).

Other writers have made further suggestions as to precisely what scaffolding is. Wood and Wood (1996a; 1996b) suggest that scaffolding comprises the overcoming of task uncertainty and contingency. A learner who is uncertain about the contours of the task, what the task entails and therefore what a proper solution to the task might be, is unlikely to be able to complete it without assistance. The expert, again assuming a process role, delineates the features of the task and this might include examples of how similar tasks have been completed, to bridge the gap between him or herself and the novice. The expert therefore has the role of reducing uncertainty; however, this does not imply that the learner is given the solution which is then internalised. What is internalised is a way of solving such tasks which can then be applied to a number of other similar tasks. The second of their principles, contingency, comprises support for the learner which involves progressively reducing the amount of control exerted by the expert until the learner is able to perform the task independently. The expert thus intervenes in the learning process in relation to the learner's needs, moving from more structured to less structured approaches until the learner performs the action without assistance.

Langer and Applebee (1986) further suggest five key factors in the scaffolding process: ownership by the learner; appropriateness of the task to the learner's stage of development; a structured approach to the completion of the task; collaboration between teacher and learner; and finally internalisation so that the learner can perform the task independently. Two other principles are relevant in this context. The first is facilitating the ability of the child to predict what will be given to them next (Palincsar and Brown, 1988); and the second is making visible the process by which the expert performs the action. Making visible the process of task completion may involve instruction where the process is revealed to the child not immediately but in a carefully staged sequence corresponding to the needs of the child. Some information for the completion of the task is not immediately made explicit.

Finally, Daniels citing Tharp (1993) suggests that scaffolding involves a number of processes:

1. Modelling: offering behaviour for imitation. Modelling assists by giving the learner information and a remembered image that can serve as a performance standard.
2. Feedback: the process of providing information on a performance as it compares to a standard. Feedback is essential in assisting performance because it allows the performance to be compared to the standard and thus allows self-correction. Feedback assists performance in every domain from tennis to nuclear physics. Offering feedback is the most common and single most effective form of self-assistance.

3. Contingency management: application of the principles of reinforcement and punishment to behaviour.
4. Instructing: requesting specific action. It assists by selecting the correct response and by providing clarity, information and decision making. It is most useful when the learner can perform some segments of the task but cannot yet analyse the entire performance or make judgements about the elements to choose.
5. Questioning: a request for a verbal response that assists by producing a mental operation the learner cannot or would not produce alone. This instruction assists further by giving the assistor information about the learner's developing understanding.
6. Cognitive structuring – 'explanations'. Cognitive structuring assists by providing explanatory and belief structures that organise and justify new learning and perceptions and allow the creation of new or modified schemata.
7. Task structuring: chunking, segregating, sequencing, or otherwise structuring a task into or from components. It assists learners by modifying the task itself, so the units presented to the learner fit into the Zone of Proximal Development when the entire unstructured task is beyond the zone.

(Tharp, 1993, pp. 271–2)

What these various writers have attempted is an adaptation of a Vygotskian perspective on the act of learning. What underpins them all, however, is a belief that the expert has the ability to solve problems in a particular way or has a certain body of knowledge which is then transferred to or assimilated by the novice.

The cultural version of the zone of proximal development comprises the merging of different elements of learning. This involves a distinction between what Vygotsky describes as scientific knowledge and everyday knowledge. In this version, the ZPD refers to the distance between the everyday experience of the child and that body of cultural knowledge which is usually thought of as the contents of the formal curriculum. Scaffolding refers to the activity of learning whereby these two are merged, and the teacher's role is to guide the learner so that informal or everyday knowledge is integrated into more formal or abstract versions of knowledge. This version of the ZPD suggests that the body of generalised knowledge is fixed and it assumes a traditional apprenticeship model whereby the learner becomes more and more expert as they absorb what is given to them.

Finally, a collectivist or societal perspective envisages a more active role for the learner, and the ZPD is defined as the distance between informal knowledge possessed by the learner by virtue of their albeit limited experiences in life and new forms of social understanding which are collectively constructed, not least during the pedagogic encounter. This more radical version of the ZPD has now moved the debate along the internalisation/participation continuum and offers a different view of pedagogy and assessment.

Practical applications

Moore (2000: 18–19) summarises Vygotsky's views on development, instruction and consciousness:

- Children's cognitive development is achieved most effectively by elaborating ideas and understandings in discussion with their teachers and peers;
- Children perform and develop better with help than without help, and ought to be given tasks that will test what is developing in them rather than what has already developed (the notion of stretching not just 'able' students, but those who may be perceived as underachieving in comparison with any accepted developmental norms);
- Children must develop 'conscious mastery' over what they have learned rather than merely being able to recite facts which may have little meaning for them;
- The development of such expertise is not subject-specific, and once acquired becomes a tool through which all learning is facilitated and enhanced.

Moore goes on to suggest that this has a number of implications for classroom practice. In order to learn a particular aspect of the curriculum, for example reading, the child needs to be ready to do so. Furthermore, children do not automatically progress to a higher stage of learning at a particular chronological age. Formal tests, whether of a diagnostic or summative type, can actually give misleading information about the child because they are conducted in environments which do not allow that child to fully express what they know and can do. Indeed, it is the active presence of adults and peers in the articulation and realisation of knowledge which allows them to express in a fundamental sense what they know. This implies a view of pedagogy which is interactive and not didactic, and which forgoes regurgitation of preconceived facts and ideas. It also implies that knowledge acquisition may be artificially restricted if confined within existing curriculum boundaries and traditional knowledge structures.

Student–teacher relations therefore need to be dialogic rather than monologic, involve collaborative learning, both with peers and the teacher, recognise learning as an active and interactive process concerned with the provisional nature of the student's knowledge and emphasise talking and writing. Jerome Bruner develops further this idea of socio-cultural learning; but in addition, in his later writings, he articulates a narrative view of knowledge.

Chapter 9

Jerome Bruner and psycho-cultural views of learning

Jerome Bruner, in his early work *The Process of Education* (1960), introduced the notion of a spiral curriculum, and this influenced his subsequent theory of mind that prioritised the social and cultural over the computational. A body of knowledge held by a child is considered to be revisable and in need of revisiting. So concepts, as in his much vaunted *Man, A Course of Study*, a curriculum project for which he provided the inspiration in the 1970s, are provisionally presented to the child and then returned to at later stages in the child's development. This has a number of implications. The notion of discrete, incremental steps through which a child progresses is replaced by the notion of the child making sense of a concept at a number of different levels and in relation to a more developed background to their learning. Instead of knowledge being understood as a fixed commodity, which is then transferred to the learner, the active and developmentally rich learner makes sense of that body of knowledge in terms of their current concerns, preoccupations and states of mind.

Bruner further highlighted three ways by which a learner transforms their experience into learning: enactive, iconic and symbolic modes. The enactive mode refers to action, the iconic to imagery and the symbolic refers to language, logic and mathematics. Bruner makes the point that learning through these three modes involves negotiation and in certain circumstances competition between them as to which is most appropriate. Though his early work focused on the development of the form that a curriculum should take, in his later work he develops a more complete theory of mind and therefore learning, which has undeniably social and cultural foundations. He describes how this theory developed:

> Some years ago I wrote some very insistent articles about the importance of discovery learning on one's own, or, as Piaget put it later (and I think better), learning by invention. What I am proposing here is an extension of that idea, or better, a completion. My model of the child in those days was very much in the tradition of the solo child mastering the world by representing it to himself [*sic*] in his own terms. In the intervening

years I have come increasingly to recognise that most learning in most settings is a communal activity, a sharing of culture. It is not just that the child must make his knowledge his own, but that he must make it his own in a community of those who share his sense of belonging to a culture. It is this which leads me to emphasise not only discovery and invention but the importance of negotiating and sharing, in a word, of joint culture creating an object of schooling and as an appropriate step on route to becoming a member of the adult society in which one lives one's life.

(Bruner, 1996, p. 127)

In this passage are encapsulated the themes that have preoccupied Bruner throughout his life: discovery learning, representation which is owned by the learner, learning being embedded in the culture and at the same time transforming that culture, and learning as a negotiated and shared activity.

Symbol-processing views of learning

Jerome Bruner distinguishes between computational or symbol-processing and socio-cultural views of learning. In typical fashion he strives to avoid taking a position in which the one is seen as the opposite of the other, so that if one position is advocated, all reference to the other is excluded.

The first of these views, the computational or symbol-processing view, understands learning as comprising coded unambiguous information about the world being sorted, stored, retrieved and managed in the same way that a computer processes data. The mind is a blank screen. Information is inputted into this device, and this information consists of pre-digested facts about the world which map onto the way the world actually works. The mind, in the act of learning, processes that information, assimilates it into the store of facts and theories that it already holds and then adjusts that worldview in the light of this new information. This is a mechanical process, with the notion of interpretation reduced to the assimilation of new information and the subsequent reformulation of the mindset of the individual. In this scenario, the individual is treated as a passive reflector of the way the world works; correct or incorrect views of the world are understood as a function of the efficiency with which these processes are conducted.

Symbol-processing approaches understand the learner and the environment as separate; learning takes place within the human mind as the individual processes information they receive through their senses, assimilates that information and creates new ways of understanding. This approach has its origins in the philosophical theory of empiricism, which understands the world as given and then received by individual minds. It separates out language from reality, mind from body, and the individual from society (Bredo, 1999). The first of these, the separation of language from reality, has a long philosophical lineage.

Hacking (1981) suggests that the traditional image of science, i.e. one based on empiricism, can be understood in the following way. There is a real world out there. This real world exists regardless of whether the observer is observing it at the time or whether it is being described as such. Furthermore, there is a correct way of describing it. Scientific theories are superior to commonsense understandings of the world. Science works by accumulating knowledge; it builds on previous understandings of the world and improves them. The ultimate purpose is to provide a complete understanding of both the natural and the social worlds. Science makes a distinction between observation and theory. Observational statements are theory-less. This leads to the idea that there are facts in the world which can be collected regardless of the belief systems of the observer. Interpretation and theory-building are second-order operations; they come out of and do not precede the accumulation of facts about the world. The correct way of conducting research is to test hypotheses developed prior to the data collection phase. Language is treated as a transparent medium; that is, words have fixed meanings, and concepts can be defined unambiguously. A distinction is usually made between how truthful statements are produced (this involves concept formation, data collection and data analysis procedures) and how they are justified. Different criteria are thought to be appropriate for each. Finally, an assertion is made that the methods which are appropriate to the natural sciences are equally appropriate to the social sciences.

The most important of the points made above is the idea that facts can be collected about the world, which are free of the value assumptions and belief systems of the collector. These facts constitute unequivocal and true statements about the world. Furthermore, learning comprises discovering what they are and developing adequate models to explain them. Winogrand and Flores (1986, p. 73), for example, suggest that the symbol-processing approach has the following characteristics:

> At its simplest, the rationalistic (i.e. symbol-processing) view accepts the existence of an objective reality made up of things bearing properties and entering into relations. A cognitive being 'gathers information' about these things and builds up a 'mental model' which will be in some respects correct (a faithful representation of reality) and in other respects incorrect. Knowledge is a store-house of representations, which can be called upon for use in reasoning and which can be translated into language. Thinking is a process of manipulating representations.

However, this implies that we can understand the world as fixed by language and that language is a transparent medium for representing reality. As Usher (1997) suggests, language, thought and learning also act to construct the world or bring it into being. This of course does not mean that an individual can create the world in any way they like; but it does suggest that the source of understanding, learning and, indeed, being resides in communities of individuals who together construct particular worlds. Furthermore, it challenges assumptions that there is a world or reality out there which is separate from our knowledge of it and that human beings have invented symbolic systems such as language and mathematical notation which mirror that reality – a view which has come to be known as representational realism – and reasserts the idea that research or learning acts to construct the world.

This notion of representational realism then misrepresents the process of how we act in relation to stimuli from our environment. Reality is not organised as such but requires the active efforts of the individual working in the world to make sense of it. The symbol-processing view of learning or mind is underpinned by this idea of representational realism. However, there is a more radical solution to the problem of the relationship between mind and reality and this is that representations of reality are given not in a prior sense because of the nature of reality, or because the human mind is constructed in a certain way, but as a result of individual human beings actively constructing that reality in conjunction with other human beings, some contemporary, some long since dead. This debate makes reference to the argument between constructivists and situated cognitivists, in that the former suggest that this active process of learning occurs in the mind, while the latter locate the process in society (Bruner, 1996). For situated cognitivists, categorising, classifying and framing the world have to be located in society and not in individual minds or in reality itself.

Symbol-processing approaches to cognition also suggest a further dualism, between mind and body. This separation of mind and body locates learning and cognition in the mind, as the mind passively receives from the bodily senses information which it then proceeds to process. The mind is conceived of as separate from the physical body and from the environment in which the body is located. Learning is understood as a passive process of acquiring information from the environment and thus this view of cognition supports didactic approaches to teaching and learning. Situated cognitivists argue that learning involves intimate and interactive contact with the environment and this both contributes to further understanding for the individual, and changes or transforms the environment itself. In other words, knowledge is not understood as a passive body of items to be learnt about the environment but as an interactive process of construction.

Finally, it is important to discuss the third dualism which critics of symbol-processing approaches have suggested is problematic. This is the separation of the individual from society. If a child or adult is given a task to do, the learner has to figure out without help what the problem is and how it can be solved. The task, moreover, is framed by a set of social assumptions made by the observer or teacher. The problem with the symbol-processing view is that an assumption is made that the task and the way it can be solved are understood in the same way by both learner and teacher. However, this is an assumption which cannot be made, and one of the consequences of making it is that the child who then fails to solve the problem is considered to be a poor learner. Rather, the child may simply have reconfigured or interpreted the problem in a way which is incongruent with that of the teacher or observer. The individual/societal distinction which is central to a symbol-processing view of cognition separates out individual mental operations from the construction of knowledge by communities of people and this leaves it incomplete as a theory of learning.

Bredo (1999, p. 32) summarises the symbol-processing approach in the following way, and at the same time indicates some of the problems with it:

> Each of these dualisms, such as the split between language and reality, mind and body, or individual and society is the product of a privileged description. Language is matched against a reality that is already described in terms of a certain vocabulary. An active agent or robot is similarly assumed to work with a certain description of the environment that is fine tuned to the problems which are likely to arise. Individuals are judged and compared in terms of an interpretation based on a fixed framework for describing what is going on. Each dualism is based on the assumption that the proper space in which things are described is known. Everything revolves around this particular centre – the unquestioned framework of an external observer. The problem, however, is that we generally don't know what the problem is in everyday life. We don't know how best to describe things or which vocabulary or orientation will be most helpful. Presupposing a particular description, vocabulary, or set of programming primitives amounts to adopting a fixed and unquestioning orientation before enquiry begins. Such a fixed orientation has blindnesses built in from the start. If the vocabulary or way of defining things can emerge from within the process of acting and inquiring, however, rather than being given from the outside, it may be changed and adapted as needed.

This symbol-processing or computational view of learning can be compared with learning theories which emphasise cultural aspects which are situated or embedded in society.

Situated or socio-cultural learning

Situated cognitive approaches were developed to solve some of the problems with symbol-processing approaches. Situated-cognition or socio-cultural theories of learning understand the relationship between the individual and the environment in a different way. They view the person and the environment as mutually constructed and mutually constructing. As a result they stress active, transformative and relational dimensions to learning; indeed they understand learning as contextualised. These contexts are: knowledge, power, teaching and learning strategies, and structures of the learning environment. The first of these is knowledge and Bruner is concerned with how such knowledge is formed by the learner through active engagement in learning.

An example from a formal learning situation will illustrate this. If a child is taught history in a formal setting such as a school, then that child is situated in particular discourses concerning gender, ethnicity, sexuality, and class, both in the subject matter of their learning and in the way that they are expected to learn what is being presented to them. Weiner (1990) for example, suggests that the United Kingdom national curriculum history syllabus is insular, chauvinistic and racially biased. She argues that it is both what is taught and what is not taught and the way what is taught is realised that constitutes discriminatory behaviour, albeit unplanned by the teachers concerned. Indeed, the teaching and learning strategy itself may be explicitly racist, again either through neglect, distortion or ideological bias. For example, curriculum materials have in the past only included pictures and diagrams of white children and neglected children of other colours. Furthermore, the child learning history is subsumed within particular learning strategies which act to organise the way they can see the world and its history. These pre-organised meanings are underpinned by particular conceptions of knowledge, ideas about what it is appropriate to learn in formal settings, and views about which aspects of the culture should be passed on from generation to generation and in what way. For example, history may be taught as a series of 'facts' about the world, and this teaching strategy is then reinforced by assessment strategies which downplay the socially constructed nature of what happened in the past. Finally, the historical knowledge which is imparted and the way in which it is taught has a history, and refers to other ways of seeing the world.

An example from an informal learning setting is learning how to be a parent. What characterises this type of learning is that there is as yet no formal type of training which a putative parent has to undergo. It is an example of learning which is situated in the activity which is the subject of the learning. The knowledge of how to bring up a child is generated from the actual practice itself. However, this is misleading because the parent at the same time is immersed in various knowledge structures which provide the context within which they make parenting decisions. First, they have memories, or at least remembered representations, of their own childhood. Second, they are surrounded by role-models, i.e. friends and members of their family, whom they may decide to emulate or perhaps react against. Third, they are offered advice about how to bring up children from a number of different sources, for example books and magazines, television programmes, relatives and friends. However, more fundamentally, they are immersed in particular discourses about parenting which act to close off other possibilities; these discourses reflect the way society is structured. Finally, putative parents have a view about themselves and how this relates to parenting. Parenting itself also takes place within particular environments, and these are structured in different ways. Single parenting is a qualitatively different experience from parenting by two or more adults. We therefore need to understand learning how to be a parent as situated and as making reference to discursive structures or significations of gender, sexuality, ethnicity, class, etc.; pre-organised meanings about parenting which reflect particular understandings about knowledge, i.e. views of childhood, adulthood, learning, identity and the like; and other viewpoints, discourses and knowledge structures which act as points of comparison. What this means is that learning is situated and that it has constructed or social features. As a result it can only be understood by making reference to those knowledge structures, discourses and practices which reflect particular time- and space-bound preoccupations of particular communities.

Furthermore, these communities are stratified in various ways. First, some individuals in society have a greater influence than others in determining what counts as legitimate knowledge and what doesn't. Second, knowledge-gathering takes place in settings and environments in which individuals have different access to resources. The subject matter of learning is in part those differences and this means that power is a necessary construct in explanations of social life. Third, there are power dimensions of the learning situation itself. This is most obvious in formal learning situations where the teacher has a greater opportunity to impose his or her version of knowledge on the learner than the learner has to construct it for themselves. However, even in the most informal of learning situations there are power dimensions present, as the learner is situated within arrangements about knowledge, how it should be organised and how it should therefore be absorbed, which act to restrict the capacity of the learner to advance their own learning. Finally, learning acts to fix reality in a particular way which is never entirely justified and cannot be legitimated by reference to a notion of what the world is really like. This act of closure itself is a part of the reality within which the learner is embedded. By adopting a particular way of working, a particular understanding of knowledge, the learner is rejecting or turning aside from other frameworks and this itself is an act of power.

However, within this general framework, learners have more control in some settings than in others. The teaching and learning strategy is constructed strongly or weakly (cf. Bernstein, 1985), where strong and weak are defined in terms of the capacity of the message system to restrict or allow different meanings, interpretations and actions. Each learning moment focuses on a particular aspect of knowledge, whether chosen by a teacher or not. This is made visible by the act of delivery. However, there are always invisible dimensions: what is not chosen and why it was not chosen are invisible.

The teaching device itself is weakly or strongly framed as well. If the teaching device is text-based, as in many forms of distance learning, it may allow the reader or learner the opportunity to interpret or read it in a number of different ways, or it limits these opportunities. On the other hand, oral commentary in the form of lectures, contributions to seminars, or contributions to tutorials by the teacher, operate in different ways. Again, this form of delivery is strongly or weakly framed. However, there are a number of differences when compared with text-based approaches. The spoken text is likely to be multi-faceted; that is, because of its greater informality and flexibility (it has not been subject to revision and redrafting) it is likely to incorporate a range of different modalities, i.e. at any one moment it may be more authoritative than at another moment. It is therefore likely to be more fragmented. Fragmentation allows a greater degree of choice because it surfaces for the attention of the student a range of possibilities from which they can then choose. The boundary between what is visible and invisible is also weakened.

The most common teaching device in formal settings involves student–teacher interchanges. Again, these may be strongly or weakly framed. If they are strongly framed, the teacher–student relationship may be such that the effect of the exchange is that the student is dispossessed of certain faulty, inadequate or insufficiently complex ideas, so that they now know or can do what was originally intended by the deliverer. However, there is another possibility, which is that the teacher does not have in mind a particular model of what the student should be able to do after the programme of study, and indeed is prepared to modify their teaching strategy in the light of what emerges. It is therefore weakly framed. The purpose of the exchanges is to dissolve, fragment or otherwise disrupt the models of knowledge held by the student and, at best, the teacher. Here, there is no attempt made to provide a replacement, since the purpose is to provide disjuncture in the minds of students, and the responsibility for replacement is devolved onto the student.

Finally, there are the structural dimensions of the learning setting itself. These comprise in part particular spatial and temporal arrangements. Distance learning approaches are constructed in particular ways so that the learner is allowed some licence for when and where they choose to study. Face-to-face teaching settings are constructed in terms of timetables, sequences of learning, particular relations between teachers and learners and organised places where the teaching takes place. All these various forms of structuring influence what is learnt, how it is learnt and how that knowledge is used in other settings and other environments. Situated-learning approaches acknowledge that these arrangements for learning are constructed by communities of people. They also suggest that learning is itself a social practice which has the potential to transform the practice itself. What this means is that learning, knowledge and its outcomes have to be understood historically and as being socially embedded.

Bruner is concerned to preserve some aspects of computationalism or symbol-processing approaches; however, his principal intent is to recover for his theory of learning the sense that it involves active meaning-making by the learner in developing categories, schema, theories and indeed facts about the world.

> It is precisely this clarity, this prefixedness of categories that imposes the most severe limit on computationalism as a medium in which to frame a model of mind. But once this limitation is recognised, the alleged struggle between culturalism and computationalism evaporates. For the meaning making of the culturalist, unlike the information processing of the computationalist, is in principle interpretive, fraught with ambiguity, sensitive to the occasion, and often after the fact.
>
> (Bruner, 1996, p. 56)

Narrative constructions of curriculum

Though Jerome Bruner in the early part of his career focused on matters directly concerned with the form that the curriculum should take, as I have suggested, his abiding interest has always been in developing a theory of mind and in particular a theory of learning. One of the more interesting routes that this has taken is an advocacy of a narrative construction of reality, and he suggests that though not difficult to grasp conceptually, it is difficult to dissect:

> We live in a sea of stories, and like the fish who (according to the proverb) will be the last to discover water, we have our own difficulties grasping what it is like to swim in stories. It is not that we lack competence in creating our narrative accounts of reality – far from it. We are, if anything, too expert. Our problem, rather, is achieving consciousness of what we do automatically, the ancient problem of prise de conscience.
>
> (Bruner, 1996, p. 147)

His solution to this problem is to adopt three strategies. The first of these is *contrast*: we listen to contrasting accounts or stories of the same event or sequence of events and compare them, with the intention of understanding how contrasting accounts of the same event can be equally coherent, and how the one can inform the other, so that a more richly textured understanding is possible. The second device he argues should be adopted is *confrontation*, where the knower is bound to examine their own version of reality in the light of superior claims made by other people defending a different version of reality or in the light of new evidence that they acquire for themselves or new ways they develop to make sense of reality. Finally, for Bruner, there is *meta-cognition*, an essential pedagogic strategy, in which the learner reflects not only on their view of reality, with the intention of changing or deepening it, but also on how they came to know it in the first place. It is thus essentially an epistemological activity, or as Bruner (1996, p. 148) puts it, 'metacognition converts ontological arguments about the nature of reality into epistemological ones about how we can know'. He further suggests that since argument or achieving shared understanding about substantive matters frequently fails, metacognition provides another strategy for the interpersonal negotiation of meaning.

These are learning strategies; however, any learning strategy has to be underpinned by an ontology, to which the learning makes reference. Bruner commits us to a theory of narrative reality and, though on the surface he would seem to be committing us to a universal ontology and epistemology for constructing the curriculum, he is conscious that there are equally, if not more, powerful epistemologies that may take precedence, even if they conflict:

> We devote an enormous amount of pedagogical effort to teaching the methods of science and rational thought: what is involved in verification, what constitutes contradiction, how to convert mere utterances into testable propositions, and on down the list. For these are the methods for creating a 'reality according to science'. Yet we live most of our lives in a world constructed according to the rules and devices of narrative.
>
> (Bruner, 1996, p. 149)

The curriculum, then, for Bruner, has to be ontologically committed to the teaching of narrative and he provides us with a number of ways of understanding the narrative form. Narrative understanding implies *a structure of committed time*. Narrative time is not chronological, in that one event or set of events comes before another and causes it. It involves individuals or communities of individuals inserting meaning into the structure of history so that conventionalised ways of understanding duration are challenged. Flashbacks, flashforwards, reinterpretations, assigning more importance than previously to insignificant events, and other recontextualising devices serve to reconstruct the past and present reality in different ways for both the narrator and the individual concerned. There is also a sense in which narrative events are reconstructed not just by individuals acting out of a sense of renewal but also in terms of the signifying elements of the context within which the individual learner is located.

Narrative reality as proposed by Bruner involves what he calls generic particularity. This relates to the existence of genres, which he argues are not 'written into the human genome' (1996, p. 134) and equally cannot be construed as cultural universals. However, Bruner suggests that they are common to all societies, even those which are unable to articulate them in a formal way. His point is that:

> No natural language that has been studied is without them: ways of conducting discourse, ways of construing the topics involved in the

discourse, speech registers and even idiolects characteristic of the discourse, often a specialised lexicon as well. We would not know how to begin construing a narrative were we not able to make an informed guess to which it belonged. Genres . . . are culturally specialised ways of both envisaging and communicating about the human condition.

(1996, pp. 135–6)

Genres are the framework within which particular aspects of a person's reality are embedded.

A further aspect of narrative construal is that narratives embody intentional states, and thus prioritise individual agency. Bruner sets his mind against the argument that reasons can also be causes, because this denies to the individual accountability for their actions. Narratives embody an active intentional view of the human condition.

Bruner argues that narratives involve hermeneutic composition, and he defines this in a particular way. No narrative text can be read in an unequivocal way, and this implies that a text can be read in a number of different ways. Further to this, the reading itself is embedded in a hermeneutical circle so that any reading that is made of a narrative text only makes sense in terms of the background to that reading. He also suggests that expert readers of narratives are not omniscient, nor can any readings be definitive.

Narratives, for Bruner, provide a source of newness, innovation and critical reflection on existing ways of understanding. He calls this implied canonicity, and argues that narratives are embedded in a canon and can be conventional, but allow us to develop a hermeneutic scepticism about received wisdom:

And so, while the creator of narrative realities links us to received conventions, he [sic] gains an extraordinary cultural power by making us consider afresh what before we took for granted. And our way of construing narrative realities – our openness to hermeneutic skepticism – makes us all the more ready to go along with the storyteller's fresh version.

(1996, p. 140)

The narrative form is open about reference in a way that a scientist's reference is not. A narrative both constructs reality and acts as a reference for it. It therefore doesn't reflect the world as it is or correspond to it, since it underpins individual meaning-making activity. Furthermore, it 'pivots on breached norms' (1996, p. 142) and is thus historically or culturally relative. It is central to changing norms, in part because it is responsible for these norms. An individual's life therefore is always constituted in and through history and in particular through different and historically relative narratives. So the individual's past is a series of iterations as cultural norms and narrative structures change over time.

For Bruner, narratives have an inherent negotiability, and can thus be contested, overwritten, reformed or reconfigured. This negotiability allows Bruner to argue that 'It may be this readiness to consider multiple narrative construals that provides the flexibility needed for the coherence of cultural life' (1996, p. 142). Moving beyond socio-cultural views of learning and in some respects in opposition to them, a further curriculum movement can be identified. Henri Giroux's advocacy of a critical form of pedagogy best exemplifies this.

Chapter 10

Henry Giroux and critical pedagogy

Henry Giroux has moved during his extensive academic career from a modernist to a post-modernist position, though he continues to reject both epistemological and ethical forms of relativism. His contribution to the field of curriculum is through his advocacy of critical pedagogy, and in his seminal book *Border Crossings: Cultural Workers and the Politics of Education* (1992) he identifies nine principles which underpin his notion of critical pedagogy.

The first of these is that educators need to focus on pedagogy as a means of reconstructing schools as democratic public spaces. He thus establishes a relationship between schooling and the wider society, both in that the one reflects the other and in that changes in pedagogy in schools will eventually result in changes in society. For Giroux: 'Education must be understood as the production of identities in relation to the ordering, representation and legitimation of specific forms of knowledge and power' (Giroux, 1992, p. 73). Thus the form this takes contributes to the way society is constructed. A critical theorist has a particular vision of society which is made manifest through the development within schools of a cadre of educated people who have developed the knowledge, skills and habits of critical citizenship, and through which democratic institutions can be reformed:

> It also means providing students with the skills they will need to locate themselves in history, find their own voices, and provide the convictions and compassion necessary for exercising civic courage, taking risks, and furthering the habits, customs, and social relations that are essential to democratic public forms.
>
> (Giroux, 1992, p. 74)

Developing appropriate pedagogies for this task is for Giroux an essential component of critical pedagogy.

The second of these principles is that critical pedagogy is an ethical project with its roots in critical theory, so that it incorporates both a vision of how society should be constructed and a theory of how currently society exploits, dehumanises and denigrates certain groups of people. Furthermore, this ethical project reflects a sense of responsibility that one should have, as Giroux describes it, to 'the other'. It has three elements: relations of power, subject positions and social practices. Each in turn has to be understood with reference to current forms of schooling and possibilities for changing those forms to better realise a socially just society.

The third principle is that, whilst celebrating difference, critical pedagogy within schools has to address the political implications of such a celebration. Teachers and students are therefore urged to engage with difference in two ways. The first of these is that student identities and subjectivities need to be understood as multiple and embedded constructs which may be contradictory, and furthermore need to be surfaced for and by students in the act of creating new, more satisfying and more socially just forms of identity. And second, critical pedagogy needs to allow students to understand how these differences between groups are embedded in history and how they can be and have been manifested in public struggles. Giroux is making the point here that the curriculum has been so constructed that its content, categories and delineations which have served to perpetuate inequality and injustice are treated as natural and thus any form of 'other' curriculum is seen as an aberration and thus to be rejected.

The fourth of Giroux's principles relates to the construction of curriculum texts and the need to avoid a master narrative that suppresses multiple interpretations. Curriculum knowledge should not be treated as a sacred text, 'but developed as part of an ongoing engagement with a variety of narratives and traditions that can be reread and reformulated in politically different terms' (1992, p. 77). He is making an epistemological point here and arguing for the possibility of a variety of readings of influential school texts and taking issue with the cultural conservative view that curriculum knowledge should be encapsulated in a canon of influential texts. This involves

> the possibility for students to creatively appropriate the past as part of a living dialogue, an affirmation of the multiplicity of narratives, the need to judge those narratives not as timeless or monolithic discourses, but as social and historical inventions that can be refigured in the interests of creating more democratic forms of public life.
>
> (1992, p. 76)

Giroux's fifth principle for critical pedagogy refers to the need to create new forms of curriculum knowledge and break down disciplinary boundaries so that new ways of thinking are not constrained by the old delineations and boundaries that divided up the corpus of knowledge. In other words, for Giroux, the current ways by which curriculum knowledge is organised serve both to contribute towards forms of discriminatory practice and in the process to conceal their historical origins. Cultural forms, embedded in curricula, need therefore to be understood as 'part of the discourse of power and inequality' (1992, p. 76).

Giroux's sixth principle addresses the issue of epistemology directly. Rationality, for Giroux, is never neutral, or as he puts it, 'reason is not innocent' (1992, p. 76). Objectivity is a cultural script that serves to give authority to a set of presuppositions that in reality are historical artefacts:

> This suggests that we reject claims to objectivity in favour of partial epistemologies that recognize the historical and socially constructed nature of their own knowledge claims and methodologies. In this way, curriculum can be viewed as a cultural script that introduces students to particular forms of reason, that structure specific stories and ways of life.
>
> (1992, p. 77)

Further to this, knowledge should be redefined so that the different ways by which groups of people learn and take up particular subject positions should be incorporated into the curriculum.

Giroux's seventh principle is an amalgam of critique and identifying possibility, and he makes clear here that his project is both political and utopian. Conditions in schools need to be created which allow students to express risky, future-orientated and hopeful thoughts. Critique itself should thus be understood not in a negative sense, but as an unravelling of the imprint of history on the essentialised and naturalised forms of language that structure curriculum-making.

His eighth principle refers to the role of the teacher, and he suggests that teachers should move away from adopting a narrow language of professionalism, and embrace a language of critique which moves beyond a 'discourse of objectivity and decentredness' (1992, p. 78), and then embrace 'a practice that is capable of revealing the historical and ideological parameters that frame its discourse and implications for the self, society, culture and the other' (1992, p. 79). Though he does not reject macro-theoretical narratives, he suggests that teachers need to operate at the local level, and locate themselves in discourses of professionalism that understand how power 'is operationalised, domination expresses itself, and resistance works in multiple and productive ways' (1992, p. 79). In effect, he adopts a Foucauldian notion of power and resistance, whilst at the same time acknowledging that powerful and totalising forces in society work to restrict attempts to create a more just and equal society.

Finally, he suggests that pedagogy should reflect the need to allow students' voices to be heard, and also that the role of the teacher is to raise the level of consciousness of their students so that they understand how their personal narratives are also embedded in wider social and political narratives – the two may of course conflict. He therefore argues that,

> To focus on voice is not meant to simply affirm the stories that students tell, nor to simply glorify the possibility for narration. Such a position

often degenerates into a form of narcissism, a cathartic experience, that is reduced to naming anger without the benefit of theorising in order to both understand its underlying causes and what it means to work collectively to transform the structures of domination responsible for social relations.

(1992, p. 80)

It is clear here that Giroux believes that current forms of schooling contribute to forms of consciousness in children which persist throughout life and which ultimately lead to the setting in place of structures that are manifestly unjust and unfair, which in turn leads to the endorsement for the next generation of forms of schooling which operate in the same way. The solution is to change these forms of ideological control that constitute current models of schooling, and replace them with forms of consciousness-raising that will lead to more just outcomes.

Transgression

Giroux expresses some sympathy with post-modern ideas, principally with the idea that individual identities are formed and re-formed in relation to shifting but still powerful discourses and structures in society. However, there is a tension in Giroux's work between the need to reject all master narratives, as a post-modernist would do, but at the same time continually to argue the case for an ethical and therefore teleological vision of society and to draw back from a rejection of all totalising explanations. To do the latter would be to deny the critical theorist the means by which to understand how individuals and groups of individuals are enmeshed in power structures which serve to oppress them:

> To reject all notions of totality is to run the risk of being trapped in particularistic theories that cannot explain how the various diverse relations that constitute larger social, political and global systems interrelate or mutually determine and constrain one another.
>
> (Giroux, 1992, p. 67)

However, he accepts that the form that language takes and how it has evolved is not necessarily oppressive; in other words, transgressive theorising can take place within the current ways that language games are being played out, and it is possible to develop more authentic representations of how power structures social life. If neo-conservatives have turned the emancipatory capacities of certain words and phrases to their own ends, then they can also be reclaimed. For Giroux, the way these language games are played out is central to how the curriculum constructs the identities of those being schooled:

At stake here is the need to make clear that language is always implicated in power relationships expressed, in part, through particular historical struggles over how established institutions such as education, law, medicine, social welfare, and the mass media produce, support, and legitimate particular ways of life that characterize a society at a given time in history. Language makes possible both the subject positions that people use to negotiate their sense of self and the ideologies and social practices that give meaning and legitimacy to institutions that form the basis of a given society.

(Giroux, 1992, p. 167)

For neo-conservatives, pedagogy, and in particular the form that pedagogy takes, is a neutral device for transmitting important values from one generation to the next, and for ensuring that society reproduces itself in an orderly way. Giroux, however, in common with Bernstein (1990), understands pedagogy as part of the production of knowledge, and thus as also implicated in how identities are produced and social relations constituted. For example, though he never develops a detailed understanding of pedagogy as a device for the transmission of knowledge and social relations, he makes clear at a general level that different forms of pedagogy produce different types of knowledge and identity in learners.

In Chapter 3 above, it was seen how Lawrence Stenhouse suggested exactly this, in his advocacy of a particular form of inquiry-based pedagogy. For Stenhouse, this constituted the best way by which children could be inducted into various forms of social discourse that in the general evolution of our culture (and codified in the disciplines) have figured prominently and significantly. Giroux therefore makes the further point that pedagogy and curriculum are not neutral devices; however, neo-conservatives may choose to conceal their ideological natures to reinforce the values which they seek to transmit:

The notion that pedagogy is itself part of the production of knowledge, a deliberate and critical attempt to influence the ways in which knowledge and identities are produced within and among particular sets of social relations, is far removed from the language and ideology of the neoconservatives.

(Giroux, 1992, p. 95)

Furthermore, he suggests that teachers who on the surface adopt critical pedagogic stances may still act in oppressive ways, if their pedagogy either unwittingly marginalises the voices of students or is underpinned by a view of knowledge which is reproductive rather than emancipatory. In effect, Giroux is suggesting that conventional authority relations in the classroom, that constitute one element of pedagogy, have to be fundamentally reconstituted to allow the voices of students to be heard. So he suggests that: 'guided by a concern with producing knowledge that is ideologically correct, radical theorists have revealed little or no understanding of how a teacher can be both politically correct and pedagogically wrong' (Giroux, 1992, p. 181). This paradox that besets all critical teachers is further expressed by Giroux in the following way:

> For many educators, pedagogy is often theorized as what is left after curriculum content is determined. In this view, knowledge 'speaks' for itself and teaching is often a matter of providing an occasion for the text to reveal itself. Guided by a concern with producing knowledge that is academically correct or ideologically relevant, educational theorists have largely sidestepped the issue of how a teacher can work from sound ethical and theoretical principles and still end up pedagogically silencing students.
>
> (Giroux, 1992, p. 98)

However, there is for Giroux an implicit assumption that certain pedagogic practices are foundational to his view as to how schools should function. These are: a respect for the views of others; the possibility of communicating; an orderly exchange of views; an acceptance that one might be wrong; and the need to be tolerant of other people's viewpoints.

Positivism

Giroux's project, set out over a number of years and in a number of books, reflects a critical theoretical perspective, grounded in the Frankfurt School and in particular Herbert Marcuse. In a seminal article (Giroux, 1979), 'Schooling and the Culture of Positivism', he provides a critique of the dominant culture of positivism, which he suggests has been concerned above all with explanation, prediction and control. Furthermore, positivist principles that underpin natural science methodology are considered to be superior to the principles of hermeneutics. Theory, for Giroux, has become in the positivist tradition exclusively concerned with those ends that are set by a pre-given empirical reality. Thus immediately we are confronted with the central theme of Giroux's work that this pre-given empirical reality has been de-historised, so that those ends and indeed the categorical distinctions that make up the social order are treated as 'natural'. Human identities are therefore always to be understood not least by those individuals themselves as searching for this pre-given norm, which science has reified as the basis for human behaviour. Giroux's critical stance treats this pre-given norm as ideology and his task is to bring about a state of affairs that allows individuals to critique and transcend their location within these ideological structures. Critical analysis has a two-fold purpose. First, it comprises an 'explosion of reification, a breaking through of mystifications and a recognition of how certain forms of ideology serve the logic of domination' (Giroux, 1997, p. 85). Second, such a critique 'must be informed by a spirit of relentless negativity, one that promotes the critical independence of the subject as well as the restructuring and transformation of an oppressive social reality' (1997, p. 86).

This has certain epistemological implications, but before we examine these, it is worth pointing to a number of consequences of adopting such a position. He insists that these social forms act to oppress individuals, and since they are located in history, they are potentially amendable. Current social arrangements do not have transcendental qualities, but are merely the results of a series of decisions made by individuals operating within mystifying practices, some of whom are alive today but many of whom are long since dead. However, Giroux wants to describe them as oppressive, which in effect means that he wants to replace them with a set of social arrangements that are less oppressive. Even if, and this is not Giroux's position, those social arrangements are concerned with process, i.e. adopting a spirit of relentless negativity, such a dispositional aim in itself cannot claim any historical transcendence. If and when those oppressive relations are consigned to the dustbin of history, and the social order can be described as not oppressive, should the individual then still operate from a position of relentless negativity? The answer is presumably that they should not, which would suggest that Giroux's post-modernist stance is always tempered by ethical and teleological elements. To be in state of non-oppression requires an acceptance that certain values and thus social arrangements have a transcendent quality.

Positivism, both as a social theory and as a methodological one, comprises a realm of objective facts which are so arranged that empirical verification is made possible and this allows law-like propositions to be developed which reflect the world as it is. Such knowledge, then, for Giroux, ignores 'the social construction of knowledge and the constitutive interests behind the selection, organisation and evaluation of "brute facts"' (1997, p. 11). Values and social positions are marginalised, and objectivity as a concept is reified and de-historised: 'what is espoused is that the very notion of objectivity is based on the use of normative criteria established by communities of scholars and intellectual workers in any given field' (1997, p. 11). His position is his-torically relative, as ideology, defined by him as those sets of ideas and concepts that structure the social world, also works on and through individuals, and in the process binds those individuals to a worldview which assents to oppressive practices within society.

Ideology

Ideological control, for Giroux, is never absolute and he criticises various forms of structural (both material and cultural) determinism. However, he argues that ideology and individual experience are connected through practices located in three areas: the unconscious, the realm of common sense and the sphere of critical consciousness. The first of these, the realm of the unconscious, is treated by Giroux not as an area in which the individual is conditioned and in which all sense of agency is lost, but as a site of both self-creation and domination. Thus the unconscious is concerned with the development of needs, which are understood as socially constructed and therefore potentially amendable, but are both repressive and emancipatory. He means by this that the unconscious can contain 'needs based on meaningful social relations, community, freedom, creative work, and a fully developed aesthetic sensibility' (1997, p. 79). He thus strengthens his argument that ideology not only functions in a monolithic way, but should be understood at the individual level of producing contradictory impulses and needs, some of which are repressive and others of which are liberatory. However, Giroux is still concerned to acknowledge 'the degree to which historical and objective societal forces leave their ideological imprint upon the psyche itself' (1997, p. 80). Thus at the cultural level, and avoiding any deterministic view of the relationship between discursive structures and agency, he argues for the development of a critical consciousness which transcends the determining effect of ideology working on individuals at the unconscious level.

The second of Giroux's ideological arenas is the area of common sense, and once again, Giroux is determined to avoid any form of cultural determinism. Lay knowledge is a repository of authentic insights into the human condition and discursive entanglements in repressive structural forms. Thus within the realm of common sense, there exists the possibility of resistance to oppressive discourses and ultimately practices, and it is only when common sense is treated in an uncritical manner that resistance becomes impossible: 'It is the grounding of common sense in an uncritical mode of mediation, a mode of mediation which is unconscious of its relation to the larger social totality, that is its singular characteristic' (1997, p. 82). Common sense is thus limited and limiting and in Giroux's terms needs to be transcended.

Finally, Giroux's third ideological arena needs to be interrogated. This refers to the interface between ideology and critical consciousness, and Giroux's take on the issue breaks decisively with neo-Marxist views of false consciousness and neo-positivist views of disparagingly comparing ideology with scientific or true knowledge. Ideology can function as a way of 'illuminating the rules, assumptions and interests that structure not only the thinking process but also the material such processes take as an object of analysis' (1997, pp. 84–5). In line with his method of critique, the normative basis for all forms of consciousness can be exposed, and human agency is allowed to float free from all forms of discursive conditioning. To be critical is to examine how the process of ideology works on oneself, is socially transformative, and admits the possibility of a radically different future. Giroux's concern then with schooling and the curriculum is to try to understand how these processes of ideological control work through a logic of domination and how a form of critical pedagogy can be embedded in curriculum structures that currently serve to oppress and discriminate.

His position furthermore is opposed to mechanistic reproduction theories, in which schooling is understood as necessarily concerned with the repro-duction of the existing order, for two reasons. (He cites Bowles and Gintis (1976) and Bourdieu and Passeron (1990) as exemplars of this type of approach.) First, within any social order, there are always possibilities for breaking this cycle of reproduction; and second, structural and indeed cultural forms should be understood as within history and thus they both endlessly reinvent themselves and operate in a dialectical relation with agency. Rather, for Giroux, schools should be seen as sites of struggle which connect the micro level of the school to the wider society:

> the notion that ideological and political structures are determined and governed by a single economic logic is rejected. Cultural and social forms contain a range of discursive and ideological possibilities that can only be grasped within the contextual and contradictory positions in which they are taken up; moreover, while such forms are reproduced under the conditions of capitalist production, they influence and are influenced by such relations.
>
> (Giroux, 1992, p. 121)

In particular, this suggests that economic or social class determinism neglects the way other markers or forms of identity, constituted in society and espe-cially through the school curriculum, have their own forms of logic, which may be in conflict with crude forms of economic determinism. So Giroux can argue that:

> Labour does not provide the exclusive basis either for meaning or for understanding the multiple and complex ensemble of social relations that constitute the wider society. In this case, social antagonisms grounded in religious, gender, racial, and ethnic conflicts, among others, possess their own dynamism and cannot be reduced to the logic of capitalist relations.
>
> (Giroux, 1992, p. 121)

Critical pedagogy

Critical pedagogy then can only operate under certain clearly defined con-ditions, and Giroux hints at some of the conditions for critical pedagogy in his book, *Pedagogy and the Politics of Hope* (1997). The first of these conditions involves a reconfiguring of the notion of authority. For conservative edu-cators, authority has a two-fold purpose: to preserve the social order by inducting children into forms of compliance which will now and in the future not threaten it; and to preserve existing cultural forms through a process of mystification that naturalises them. Since the social order is racist, sexist, discriminatory and unjust, then this social order needs to be overturned. For Giroux, it means that a new language has to be invented to do just that and an emancipatory authority is what is called for. Such a normative position is commonplace in Giroux's writings as he always seeks to displace commonsense and accepted meanings of key terms for and by curriculum scholars:

> the concept of authority like any social category of importance has no universal meaning waiting to be discovered. As a subject of intense battles and conflicts among competing theoretical perspectives, its meaning has often shifted depending on the theoretical context in which it has been employed. Given these shifting meanings and associations, it becomes necessary in any attempt to redefine the centrality of authority for a critical pedagogy to interrogate the way in which the concept has been treated by preceding ideological traditions.
>
> (Giroux, 1997, p. 97)

Giroux's notion of emancipatory authority then allows teachers to see themselves, and be seen, as transgressive intellectuals who shape curriculum content and pedagogy so that dominant ways of thinking and acting are challenged. This necessarily involves the reorganisation of those structures within which they work so that they are allowed a measure of independence and are not constrained by forms of authority which perpetuate the existing social order. In other words, an emancipatory authority for a teacher carries with it the imperative to critique and indeed reject those authorial approaches which reinforce divisions of labour in society and disempower teachers and students. The link is established between thinking and acting critically and transforming society. The danger is that if traditional forms of authority within which students have been embedded for most of their lives are undermined, the conditions for allowing students to challenge those traditional discursive and structural forms which make up the curriculum cannot be met. In order to effect such a radical zeitgeist, disorder is likely to ensue. Diagnosing the problem is a different activity from reconfiguring existing arrangements that have oppressive consequences. One only has to observe how radical educators behave in their own academies when placed in positions of authority; rarely is that authority seen as emancipatory.

Giroux is aware of the difficulties and in a sense what he is proposing is a utopian model, which specifies the conditions for its enactment. So

> it is important to stress that unless teachers have both the authority and the power to organise and shape the conditions of their work so that they can teach collectively, produce alternative curricula, and engage in emancipatory politics, any talk of developing and implementing

progressive pedagogy ignores the reality of what goes on in the daily lives of teachers and is nonsensical.

(1997, p. 107)

The second specific transgressive activity that Giroux argues for in his discussion of the shape and form of a radical pedagogy is the need to read texts critically, and in particular those cultural artefacts that are produced and used in classrooms. This suggestion by Giroux locates the critical at the pedagogic level, though such a type of reading would also apply to the texts and scripts that teachers themselves are embedded within as representatives of the existing social order.

> This means providing the learning opportunities for students to become media-literate in a world of changing representations. It means offering students the knowledge and social relations that enable them to critically read not only how cultural texts are regulated by various discursive codes, but also how such texts express and represent different ideological interests.

(Giroux, 1992, p. 135)

Critical textual reading in line with the general epistemological thrust of Giroux's work has a number of elements. The curriculum text has to be treated as a social construct, embedded in history, and therefore capable of being read within a number of other texts and structural forms; or at least texts, and this would include canons of literature, should not have attached to them universal and transcendental meanings. They can be deconstructed as historically embedded artefacts.

A further critical pedagogic form is that such texts are read, disputed and discussed through locating the contradictions and aporias within them and in the process identifying the sets of interests that allow them within traditional pedagogic forms to be treated as legitimate and authoritative. The text needs to be read through the way it is constructed, its formal, semantic and grammatical elements, which allow students to understand how they have become and can become empowered and constrained by particular textual devices, and how this opens up and closes off particular ways of seeing the world. The text also needs to be read as a mystifying document that seeks through its various authoritative devices to silence particular voices and to reposition them as marginal. Finally, and this is typical of Giroux's general approach, the text has to be read as an empowering document, opening up possibilities and new insights about how the social world is constructed. We can see here how texts, and indeed structural forms, for Giroux are always sites of contestation, and thus have both empowering and constraining elements. However, texts and scripts may refer to both the form that the pedagogic encounter takes and the artefact that constitutes the object of deliberation. Again, there is the possibility that within the pedagogic encounter, a gap develops between the mode of delivery and the type of treatment accorded to the object being investigated. An authoritative approach to a critical reading of key texts, supported by state-sanctioned evaluative processes and systems of power that privilege the knowledge of the teacher, is likely to render the efforts of the teacher redundant.

The third critical pedagogic form that Giroux endorses relates to the way the experience of students is mediated within schools. For Giroux, a critical pedagogy has to acknowledge those ways of making sense of the world which structure the lives of students; and 'the discourse of lived culture should interrogate the ways in which people create stories, memories and narratives that posit a sense of determination and agency' (1992, p. 140). This is the starting point for the development of a radicalised consciousness in students and it is only through this process that students can begin to engage with the contradictory nature of their experience and more importantly how their experience is mediated through public and state-sponsored discourses. Giroux describes this process as one of self-production, and it involves a critical interrogation of three types of voices that emerge from three different ideological sites within the school: the dominant and officially sanctioned voice of the school, the student's own voice, and the voice of the teacher.

For Giroux, the curriculum is a socially constructed artefact, with the implication that good reasons need to be provided to justify the prescriptive model that is proposed. Instrumentalist views of the curriculum can take an economistic or humanist form. Donald Schon's work on reflective activity provides one possible rationale for the curriculum.

Chapter 11

Donald Schon and reflection

Donald Schon focused on a number of issues central to the study of the curriculum, and in particular foregrounded the importance of reflection in the learning process. A computational model of learning suggests that the learner passively receives stimuli from the environment and then assimilates them into their existing frameworks of understanding. Learning theorists, such as Jerome Bruner (1996), have generally been dissatisfied with this model of learning and have argued for an interactive process of assimilation, with the capacity of the human agent to reflect on what they receive from their environment and in the process change it. Structures, whether in the form of dispositions, habits or practices, or as 'properties of social entities' (Nash, 2005), may become reified unless agency and reflection are given prominence in any model of learning.

Schon's reflective model focused specifically on professional practice and how the practitioner learns in workplace settings. He argued that current ways of understanding such learning emphasise problem-solving rather than problem-setting, so that the problem is reconstituted and seen as different and new.

> From the perspective of Technical Rationality, professional practice is a process of problem *solving*. Problems of choice or decision are solved through the selection, from available means, of the one best suited to established ends. But with this emphasis on problem solving, we ignore problem *setting*, the process by which we define the decision to be made, the ends to be achieved, the means which may be chosen. In real-world practice, problems do not present themselves to the practitioner as givens. They must be constructed from the materials of problematic situations which are puzzling, troubling and uncertain.
>
> (Schon, 1983, pp. 39–40)

In this seminal passage from *The Reflective Practitioner* (1983) he makes the point that real learning in practice settings is more than just problem-solving. Further to this, he suggests that most of our knowledge as it relates to action, or knowledge-in-action, is implicit. In other words, it does not involve conscious processes, so that actions, recognitions and judgements are skilled activities which are carried out spontaneously and the individual learner is not aware of them while seeking solutions to problems encountered.

Any action therefore has a background which is implicit in that action. It is not just that the learner knows what to do, it is also that the knowledge itself that underpins the action is socially embedded and has become so through previous cycles of learning which may or may not have involved conscious reflection. Schon (1983, p. 54), for example, argues that:

> In some cases, we were once aware of the understandings which were subsequently internalized in our feeling for the stuff of action. In other cases, we may never have been aware of them. In both cases, however, we are usually unable to describe the knowing which our action reveals.

Having suggested that most actions do not involve the activity of reflecting on those actions and what motivated them, Schon also identifies a class of actions which he describes as meta-reflective, that is, the background to the action is made explicit through a further process of contemplation and reflection. This further process may take two forms: reflecting on the action and its consequences or reflecting on the activity which produced the action.

Reflection-in-action

What form might this reflection-in-action take? Schon begins the process of answering this question by suggesting a paradox. Though most new situations that a learner is confronted with are perceived to be unique in the first instance, to make sense of them the learner has to try to fit them into their existing framework of rules and resources, and they do this by looking for similarities and differences.

> When a practitioner makes sense of a situation he [sic] perceives to be unique, he sees it as something already present in his repertoire. To see this site as that one is not to subsume the first under a familiar category or rule. It is, rather, to see the unfamiliar, unique situation as both similar to and different from the familiar one, without at first being able to say similar or different with respect to what. The familiar situation functions as a precedent, or a metaphor, or – in Thomas Kuhn's phrase – an exemplar for the unfamiliar one.
>
> (Schon, 1983, p. 138)

Schon understands the process of learning as cyclical with successive iterations of comparing new and familiar experiences with well-established routines of thinking, many of which the learner may have difficulty with bringing to consciousness.

Schon then introduces a new activity, which he calls experimentation, as the learner interacts with their environment and attempts to make sense of it. Three processes are involved: exploring the possibilities inherent in the problem; developing a series of action steps and testing them out to see if they fit the problem and thus work; and finally, evaluating the more successful solutions to develop working hypotheses. These three processes are, for Schon, non-sequential but implicated in what he describes as experimenting in practice.

> When the practitioner reflects-in-action in a case he [*sic*] perceives as unique, paying attention to phenomena and surfacing his intuitive understanding of them, his experimenting is at once exploratory, move testing, and hypothesis testing. The three functions are fulfilled by the very same actions. And from this fact follows the distinctive character of experimenting in practice.
>
> (Schon, 1983, p. 150)

Experimenting in practice, however, is both reflective and transactional. It is not a passive process because the learner is both testing out new hypotheses, extending their rich store of knowledge about how to go on in life and seeking to change the external setting in which the problem is embedded. Change therefore operates at two levels, the psychological and the social.

> Their hypothesis-testing experiment is a game with the situation. They seek to make the situation conform to their hypothesis but remain open to the possibility that it will not. Thus their hypothesis-testing activity is neither self-fulfilling prophecy, which ensures against the apprehension of disconfirming data, nor is the neutral hypothesis testing of the method of controlled experiment, which calls for the experimenter to avoid influencing the object of study and to embrace disconfirming data. The practice situation is neither clay to be moulded at will nor an independent, self-sufficient object of study from which the inquirer keeps his [*sic*] distance. The inquirer's relation to this situation is *transactional*. He shapes the situation, but in conversation with it, so that his own models and appreciations are also shaped by the situation. The phenomena that he seeks to understand are partly of his own making; he is in the situation that he seeks to understand. This is another way of saying that the action by which he tests his hypothesis is also a move by which he tries to effect a desired change in the situation, and a probe by which he explores it. He understands the situation by trying to change it, and considers the resulting changes not as a defect of experimental method but as the essence of its success.
>
> (Schon, 1983, pp. 150–1)

The experimental method is not designed to produce generalisable knowledge about problem-solving, learning and how to go on in life, but comprises an endless series of iterations of reflection and action. Schon does, however, suggest that such knowledge may be generalised and generalisable in certain circumstances, but only in so far as it contributes to the store of knowledge held by the learner, which they can then call on as background in future action-reflection cycles.

> Reflection-in-action in a unique case may be generalised to other cases, not by giving rise to general principles, but by contributing to the practitioner's repertoire of exemplary themes from which, in the subsequent cases of his [*sic*] practice, he may compose new variations.
>
> (Schon, 1983, p. 140)

Schon's description of reflection-in-action is supplemented by a further notion of reflection on reflection-in-action, and we need to address this as it relates to formal learning and transfer of learning from the classroom to real-life settings.

Single- and double-loop learning

Reflection and reflective practices are central to the development of a learning theory. Argyris and Schon (1978) distinguish between theories-in-use and espoused theories: theories-in-use refer to the type of reflection that takes place within the daily activity of the practitioner – theories-in-action – and espoused theories comprise reflection and articulation of those theories-in-action to other interested parties. This articulation and subsequent theorisation of reflection-in-action involves an extension and reconfiguring of the original process of reflection.

They make a further distinction between single-loop and double-loop learning, with single-loop learning being defined as reflection about the loop between the action strategy and actions which result from it, and double-loop learning involving reflection on the purposes, frameworks and values that underpin the work of the organisation, which Argyris and Schon (1978, pp. 2–3) call 'governing variables':

> When the error detected and corrected permits the organisation to carry on its present policies or achieve its present objectives, then that error-and-correction process is *single-loop* learning. Single-loop learning is like a thermostat that learns when it is too hot or too cold and turns the heat on or off. The thermostat can perform this task because it can receive information (the temperature of the room) and take corrective action. *Double-loop* learning occurs when error is detected and corrected in ways that involve the modification of an organisation's underlying norms, policies and objectives.

The distinction between single- and double-loop learning is integral to Schon's subsequent articulation of reflection-in-action. Both types of learning taken together provide the foundations for a theory of reflection; what they do not do is account for triple-loop learning, in that the practitioner, far from being isolated within the workplace, is also influenced by external forces. This is especially relevant in the case of the student practitioner who is required to import ideas into their own practice. Single-loop reflection-in-action, then, is a process in which the learner identifies a problem, works out a possible solution, tests it, evaluates whether it can work, and embeds this new practice into their repertoire. It then becomes a routine part of their day-to-day activity. It is only referred to again if it is relevant to solving a new problem; however, identifying the problem and the solution to that problem is always located within tacit and therefore unexamined assumptions held by the learner about the organisational structures, power relations, purposes and values of the workplace setting itself. It is situation-specific, cannot be applied to other settings, expands the knowledge repertoire of the practitioner, and is oral, impermanent and not formally codified.

Double-loop reflection-in-action involves a further process of reflection in that the practitioner explicitly focuses on wider concerns so that the problem and its solution are framed by organisational structures and, indeed, political and social structures which are external to the organisation itself but impact on it. The direction of the loop is non-linear and multi-directional, and may involve a visiting and revisiting of the various parts of the model until the learner comes up with a solution. What this implies is that the action part of the reflection has wider implications than the immediate workplace practices of the learner.

Schon identifies a further stage, which he calls reflection on reflection-in-action. At this stage reflective work is performed on reflections already made, with the result that a meta-process is set in motion. With this meta-process, the emphasis shifts to the reflective activity that was an implicit part of the reflection-in-action. And this process may lead to a third type of learning, which Flood and Romm (1996) have called triple-loop learning. I have already suggested that double-loop learning may not take a linear form, and this applies to triple-loop learning as well. Its influence therefore may be multi-directional and each site is implicated to different degrees at different moments. For example, the focus of activity may be at practice, institutional or extra-institutional levels; and, depending on which level, a different type of action may result. Further to this, the level at which the practitioner is focusing will determine how the problem is treated, and whether the learner sets in motion a process of re-naming and re-framing of the problem. Indeed, the problem may within this process no longer come to be seen as a problem and the learner is not required to find a solution to it; though it is more likely that this meta-process will provide the learner with a different type of problem requiring a different type of solution. In short, this extends the complexity of the model, because reflection on reflection-in-action may lead to either an unreflexive process of change (the production of technicist knowledge); or to a critical perspective and thus radical change (depending on circumstances and thus leading to the development of critical forms of knowledge); or to a detached form of understanding which has no immediate relationship to action (and has direct affinities with disciplinary forms of knowledge).

(Scott *et al.*, 2004, p. 63)

Triple-loop learning, then, focuses critically on both the internal dynamics of the workplace, the way the student-practitioner is positioned by intra- and extra-institutional discourses, and those external factors that serve to define the institution itself (cf. Flood and Romm, 1996). However, learning involving the importation of ideas, and reflection on structures, may also be technicist as well as critical.

Meta-reflection

Reflective activity may be near to or distanced from the object of reflection, and this is best illustrated by the difference between reflection-in-action and reflection on reflection-in-action. This meta process of reflecting on a prior process of reflection can be construed in a number of ways and more importantly can take a number of different directions. The direction for the reflective process can be from practice to articulation to meta-theorising about that reflection or about the activity or about the consequences of that activity; or the original impetus for the subsequent reflection comes from outside the workplace setting and is then imported into it, subsequently influencing it. Furthermore, it is usual for the direction of the reflective activity to take a complicated form, so that reflection in action, reflection about reflection in action, and meta-reflection about the activity and subsequent reflection which now inheres in it may operate so that reflection-in-action promotes meta-reflection or meta-reflection is prior to reflection about reflection-in-action and so forth. It would be misleading to suggest that these three forms of reflection operate in a uni-directional, linear fashion.

There are, however, still a number of problems with incorporating a notion of meta-reflection into the curriculum. Schon's work principally focused on extra-formal learning; however, the notion of meta-reflection – reflecting on the process by which knowledge is acquired – as a component of the school curriculum has some merit. In relation to workplace learning, transfer between meta-reflection and action is closely related; in the case of children, far removed in time from those practice contexts. Even then, if we make an assumption that reflection is a virtue in its own right, we may still decide that meta-reflection actually impedes better performance outside the learning setting; and as a consequence we may decide that unreflective skills acquisition is a better preparation for life and a sounder basis for education than having knowledge of the process by which we acquire knowledge. On the other hand, if we decide that this process of meta-reflection enhances the application of skills outside the classroom and in relation to leading a fulfilled life, then we may be inclined to argue on instrumentalist grounds that meta-reflection should form an essential part of the skills base of any curriculum.

There is a further complication, which is that this meta-process may cause the student to know more about their practice, but the purpose is not change or improvement to that practice, but more profound understandings of the external world. Indeed, it is feasible to suggest that these deeper under-standings may lead to the student becoming less able to go on life. It is possible to imagine a situation in which reflection either causes the learner to surface such knowledge and therefore become more self-conscious, resulting in less spontaneous actions and behaviours and therefore less effective practice; or wider and deeper understandings of what the learner is doing may lead him or her to question the moral basis of their actions so that they are less likely to be able to live effectively.

In formal learning, instances of meta-reflection are commonplace, though they tend to take a reductionist form, i.e. the student is asked to reflect on their progress against a set of descriptors provided for them from an external source, and then plan and execute action steps with the intention of improving their performance. This is a limited form of meta-reflection, and suffers from the disadvantage that the student may feel that they do not own the process, and that the set of descriptors are not written at the required level of particu-larity to enable them to improve their performance. Schon's (1987) criticism of technical rationality, as we will see, requires the learner, whether in formal or post-compulsory settings, to move beyond the implementation of know-ledge and protocols developed by external agencies to a situation where the practitioner/user both is implicated in that process of knowledge development and uses it in their practice settings.

Technical rationality

Reflective practices have become central to professional development courses in the early twenty-first century, especially as courses are constructed with the aim of integrating practitioner experience, workplace learning and academic study. Incorporating these reflective practices into the repertoires of students has occasioned some criticisms. These focus on the affective dimension of learning so that students are not encouraged to explore 'inner discomforts' (Brookfield, 1987); the technicist nature of the reflective activity undertaken (Boud and Walker, 1998); the unreflexive and decontextualised form of this reflective behaviour (Usher et al., 1997); the lack of criticality implicit in the reflective activity; and the uncritical acceptance of experience as the driver for change within the workplace (Boud and Walker, 1998).

Many of these criticisms were inspired by Schon's (1983; 1987) powerful attack on what he called technical rational knowledge. Practitioners are required to set to one side their own considered and experience-based ways of conducting themselves at work because these are partial, incomplete and subjective; by contrast they incorporate into their practice scientific knowledge that transcends the local and the particular. Practitioner knowledge is therefore considered to be inferior and incomplete because it is context-dependent, problem-solving, contingent, non-generalisable and judged not by objective criteria but by whether it contributes to the achievement of short-term goals and problems encountered in situ. An assumption is made that the objective knowledge that is produced about programmes, activities and institutions binds the practitioner in particular ways, namely the following of rules which can be deduced from that knowledge. Knowledge produced by outsiders, or by practitioners behaving as outsiders, is superior to the knowledge produced by practitioners working in situ.

The implication for workplace learners is that they should divest themselves of their prior incorrect and incomplete knowledge and adopt precepts based on the objective study of practical activities. Usher *et al.* (1997) describe the activity of the practitioner in this mode as technical and problem-solving. It is a view that is concerned with establishing a measure of technical efficiency that will necessarily lead to the achievement of predetermined ends which are separate from the determination of means per se. Lyotard (1984) has argued that knowledge is now constructed and legitimated in terms of its capacity to enhance the efficiency and effectiveness of the economic and social system. He is suggesting that those forms of knowledge which have their roots in a foundationalist epistemology no longer have credibility in society, and have been replaced, in the current conditions of post-modernity, by knowledge as the optimising of efficient performance.

Knowledge in this mode is applied to the practice setting, and indeed its rationale is whether it makes the workplace a more efficient and a more productive place. Such knowledge may refer to the skill development of the individual, i.e. presentational skills; or to the strategic knowledge the individual needs to function effectively in the workplace; or to the technical ability of the individual who then can better provide the workplace with solutions to problems encountered there. There is no desire here to examine the various contexts of the work, whether they are political, ethical or consequential. The main criterion for the successful development of this process is whether it works in practice.

Technical rational knowledge, then, has been criticised by Schon for marginalising the role of the implementer, for its failure to understand how knowledge is acquired in workplace settings and for the frequently crude and reductionist form it takes. In its place, Schon has argued that knowledge is and should be concerned with framing and reframing problems encountered in situ, reflective and in certain circumstances meta-reflective activity, and its production as a skilled activity by the learner.

I identified previously a number of forms that reflection could take and indeed was taking in the various curriculum contexts that I have focused on. These were: reflection-in-action as problem-solving; reflection on reflection-in-action; reflection on reflection-in-action which then leads to planned change to practice; reflection-in-action as the re-naming and re-framing of practice; and meta-reflection which engages with the process of reflection itself. Schon's (1983) critique of technical rationality still has some resonances with the types of knowledge created by student-practitioners engaged in learning processes, whether of an informal or formal kind. He suggested that learning should take a reflective turn:

> When we attend to what we know already, appreciating the artistry and wisdom implicit in competent practice, believing that by reflection on that practice we can make some of our tacit knowledge explicit, we take a 'reflective turn' that leads us to see students and teachers (at their best) as participants in a kind of reflective practice, a communicative and self-reflective practice of reciprocal enquiry.
>
> (Schon, 1992, p. 127)

Other virtues than reflection, such as the development of imagination (cf. Greene, 1973; 1978; 1988; 1995), have been suggested as candidates for inclusion in any curriculum rationale. A more fully developed model of the virtues that it is argued should underpin a curriculum – a version of humanist instrumentalism – is discussed in the next chapter. This focuses on the notion of autonomy, and is best exemplified in the work of John White.

Chapter 12

John White on autonomy

John White provides a different rationale for the curriculum, which is neither foundationalist nor conventionalist. He argues that it is possible to identify certain virtues or dispositions that children should have in order to lead a fulfilled life. This is in contrast to narrow views of the purposes of schooling such as economism, where the single and only end-point is the efficient working of the economy. However, White's project is a different one, and, though still instrumentalist, understands the purposes of education as relating to the whole life of the person, as they are being educated and as they are living that life. This approach is problematic in two ways: individuals may disagree about what constitutes a fulfilled life; and curriculum-makers may not be able to establish which particular experiences would lead to the development of dispositions that allow the individual to lead a fulfilled life once they have been educated (cf. Callan, 1988; Clayton, 1993).

White (1982) has argued, as an underpinning rationale for the curriculum, for a notion of autonomy or the capacity to reflect on experience and make wise choices; and, further to this, that if the person is unable to make such choices or to develop such capacities, they will be unable to distinguish between projects they should pursue which contribute towards a fulfilled life and projects which do not. He takes the argument one step further by suggesting that, if they do not develop such capacities, they are liable to be in thrall to arbitrary authority, and he is thus making an assumption that it is possible to distinguish between cases of arbitrary and legitimate authority. It may also be difficult to distinguish between actions which have been motivated by conformity to an arbitrary authority and actions that have genuinely resulted from the exercise of autonomy, not least by the person themselves, since that person may argue that what looks on the surface to be conformity to an arbitrary authority is in fact freely willed.

This dilemma for White reflects a tension between leading an autonomous life and leading a fulfilled one, and the one should not be equated with the other. Someone who indulges their appetites may not be considered to be autonomous; however, they might want to argue that this is what they have freely chosen to do, and that this therefore is an expression of their autonomy.

It is here that the problem is at its starkest because autonomy as a concept has attached to it in everyday speech a series of implicit and normative meanings. Autonomy means more than making choices or even having the capacity to make choices. There is a sense in which it is used to indicate the making of good or right choices and this is reflected in White's distinction between self-regarding reasons for choosing one form of life over another and other-regarding reasons in which the person also contributes to the welfare of others. Instrumentalist views of curriculum-making are future-orientated, and can therefore only be justified with reference to utopian and normative political and social arrangements, and these are likely to be contested.

A curriculum rationale

Justifications for including some items in the curriculum and excluding others can be made in terms of instrumentality; that is, education is the sine qua non of leading the good life. The problem is then two-fold: first, to determine and provide a justification for the good life and, second, to determine the type of educational provision which will result in children, after they have been educated, leading the good life. It is possible to qualify this further by suggesting that in determining the curriculum, those experiences provided for children which will best lead to the achievement of the good life may become redundant, since the ability of those children to lead the good life is contingent upon future social and political arrangements in society which are emergent or changing. For example, in times of full employment, the majority of adults stay in the same or similar jobs throughout their careers. In times of high unemployment, this cannot be guaranteed, so, in order to lead the good life adults need to be able to adapt to changing circumstances and be more flexible in the job market. The dispositions that inhere in the curriculum prescriptions of one era may be irrelevant in another. What constitutes the good life therefore may be ephemeral and should not be treated as a fixed commodity in order to determine those educational experiences for a particular group, cohort or generation of children.

The second qualification is that this argument sets up an artificial distinction between a period of childhood and a period of adulthood. It is artificial because curriculum designers may also be concerned with the good life for children as they are learning how to be adults. So, for example, it is possible to suggest that children should be provided with certain experiences which allow them to develop dispositions that in turn will allow them when they become adults to lead the good life, having first established that in fact such dispositions do lead to this desired state of affairs; but then to reject the inculcation of such dispositions on ethical grounds. This involves a rejection of the use of certain pedagogic approaches, even though in the long term it is known that they will better enable the child to experience the good life as an adult.

The third qualification is more problematic. Children have different life courses, different dispositions and different levels of cultural capital. Curriculum theorists may therefore decide that in order for most people to enjoy the good life, because it is not possible for everyone to enjoy it, they are prepared to forgo, on strict utilitarian grounds, the possibility of some groups or members of the population ever achieving that good life. They might indeed decide that the good life is only achievable for a proportion of the population and they therefore have to decide what that proportion should be. Various criteria for determining this have been suggested and used in the past, such as selection on merit, through birthright, by income, through effort, by geographical area or by ethnic background, gender, or whatever. In order to justify such a selection, a pre-judgement has been made that the good life, or the degree to which the good life can be achieved for everyone, has to be rationed.

The good life is a generic phrase which points to an ideal state, rarely achieved by anyone and more importantly rarely achieved by anyone all the time. However, putting to one side for the time being the difficulties associated with defining what it is, it is still possible to talk, again in utilitarian terms, about achieving the good life for as many people as possible. This implies a variety of good lives, which are different for different people and groups of people, all of which in combination comprise the end-point of what society is trying to achieve. The curriculum theorist therefore has to work out the best means for achieving this, and in part this will consist of educating children into a certain way of life, which at this stage they may not fully understand as the most appropriate set of dispositions, knowledge attributes or skills for them.

First- and second-order dispositions

A way out of this dilemma or series of dilemmas is to frame those dispositions, knowledge agendas or skills not in terms of actually leading the good life but in terms of the ability to make choices that might lead to such fulfilment. Here, a distinction is being made between the development of dispositions and knowledge that then allows a person to make the appropriate choices with regard to leading a fulfilled life at a later point in time, and those which directly contribute to its achievement. This can be expressed as a distinction between first-order and second-order dispositions, and the justification for including them in the curriculum rests with an argument in favour of the first set of dispositions, because, though they may in fact never lead to the acquisition of the second set of dispositional virtues, this is the intention.

First-order dispositions are personal characteristics such as autonomy, deliberation, reflection and sound judgement about consequences, which cannot be justified as ends in themselves; but they are justified because they allow individuals to lead the good life. Second-order dispositions are of a different type because here if the person has acquired these characteristics, then in their performance they are actually leading the good life. First-order dispositions may also become second-order dispositions: for example, a person who chooses to lead a contemplative life, consisting of the exercise of autonomy, deliberation and reflection, will use both first- and second-order dispositions. Examples of second-order dispositions might be being well disposed towards other people because this brings satisfaction in its own right, or the development of athletic skills because these again may give satisfaction and contribute to the good life. A further qualification needs to be made and this is that exercising these first-order dispositions or characteristics, even in the most effective way, will not necessarily lead to the fulfilled life being achieved, and this is because that achievement may be contingent upon a whole raft of factors outside a person's control.

The reason for distinguishing between first-order and second-order dispositions or virtues is that second-order dispositions are too numerous to be developed in a single person's lifetime, and therefore choices have to be made between them. In order to make those choices, first-order dispositions have to be framed so that they focus on the capacity of the individual to distinguish between them. For example, a person who is not autonomous because he or she does not know how to exercise autonomy, cannot make an appropriate choice. The choice they make or think that they have made is not a real choice, because such a choice has to be made in terms of all the various options available to that person, and if that person does not know about those alternatives, or has not acquired the skill to make a judgement between them, then the choice they make cannot be a real one. This needs to be qualified in so far as no one has complete knowledge of all the options, so all choices are limited to some degree.

Effective choice-making has three characteristics. First, the individual has to have a sound and reliable knowledge of the present, i.e. they have to understand the balance of constraints and enablements within which they are embedded as social beings. Second, they need to have developed a knowledge of the self, their beliefs, dispositions and characteristics, so that in projecting themselves into the future (any choice is by definition about what might happen to them at some future time point) they can make a realistic evaluation of the consequences of the choice that they are making. Third, they need to have the capacity to make a judgement about the consequences of their actions, as any choices which they do make are always circumscribed by choices that other people make, and affect the choices that they might want to make in the future. This entails knowledge of the self, and the attached disposition is the capacity to use that knowledge so that they make wise choices and exercise their autonomy.

The paradox that inheres in this is that in order for the chooser to make the right choice for themselves, and to exercise their autonomy, they may have to learn and be taught how to exercise their autonomy in conditions which involve restrictions on their autonomy. And this is only a paradox if it is accepted that the educated individual by definition can act autonomously or have the capacity to make choices. A justification therefore for this disposition has to be provided. The argument that I have set out so far does not prescribe what that good life might be or indeed what those choices should be. And it may be that the choice made by the individual involves them in refusing to make choices or in not exercising their autonomy. However, they cannot logically refuse to make choices or not exercise their autonomy unless they have the capacity to do so in the first place. The latter is prior to the former, and the only way to counter this is to suggest that making choices or exercising one's autonomy is not central to the human condition.

Autonomy

White, in arguing for autonomy, is also aware of some of the problems with this argument:

> It is a popular thesis of contemporary philosophy that the individual's good consists in the satisfaction of those desires which, *on reflection*, he [*sic*] prefers to satisfy, given a full understanding of all the possible options (Rawls, 1971, ch. 7). Educationally, this generates the aim of equipping the pupil to work out what he most prefers to do, e.g. by providing him with an understanding of different ends-in-themselves and seeing that he develops the disposition to make reflective and therefore autonomous choices.
>
> (White, 1973, p. 39)

White identifies a number of problems with this viewpoint. The first of these is that there are many preferred ends and thus many autonomous choices. So, if an individual has chosen to spend their life in front of the television, the argument for autonomy cannot allow a judgement to be made about this choice, so long as it was a genuinely autonomous choice, and the only conclusion that can be reached is that a life lived in front of a television is no better or worse than one lived as a scholar engaged in trying to understand the world. Indeed, the individual may choose to exercise autonomy by refusing to be autonomous. If we accept this position, then, with the limited exception of the disposition of being autonomous or self-reflective, this does not provide a means to determine that some activities should be included in the curriculum at the expense of others. Thus, musical appreciation is given equal status to gluttony. In other words, we have to find another, and external, justification for including some items in the curriculum at the expense of others.

There is a further problem with equating autonomy with choice-making per se, and this is that making certain choices at one point in time necessarily impacts on the individual's capacity to make choices at some future point in time. So, for example, it is possible to argue that if that person makes poor choices at some stage in their life, then this will prevent them (because they develop dispositions and habits as a result of what they do in life and as a result of the choices that they have previously made) from exercising their autonomy in the future. I have already defined autonomy in three ways: sound and reliable knowledge of the present, a knowledge of the self, and the capacity to make a judgement about the consequences of one's actions. If in the making of choices, a person is restricting or limiting their capacity to make future choices by, for example, reducing their capacity to be able to make a judgement about the consequences of their actions, then in effect they are not exercising their autonomy. Though this argument has some merit, there are still some problems with it. First, we can have no absolute knowledge of the effects of choices that we make. At the time of making the choice, all we can do is speculate about its consequences. This does not rule out the possibility of making a judgement about some choices being better than others on the grounds that those choices will not restrict our ability to make choices in the future, whereas other choices might do so, because the argument does not rest on the making of perfect choices in the first place, only that some choices are better than others, and that we can only really know which is which at some later point in time. However, we can still speculate about the quality of the choice that we do in fact make in terms of whether in the future it is going to restrict us in making further choices or enhance our choice-making. The second problem is that the good life is being exclusively equated with the making of choices or the exercising of autonomy, and this rules out the evident satisfaction we might gain from meeting certain primitive and innate appetites.

White's (1982, p. 40) second argument against autonomy is to suggest that it is difficult to

> distinguish between two interpretations of the claim that the individual should autonomously choose his [sic] own way of life. (1) The first allows him autonomously to choose to be non-autonomous: after careful reflection, he decides to follow a life of servitude. (2) The second demands that the way of life he chooses embodies autonomy within it: it is not something he can ever cast off.

I have already suggested one possible reason why his first interpretation might not fit with the extended notion of autonomy that we are working with. A life of servitude is likely to reduce our capacity to make meaningful choices in the future. The second for White is more problematic, as he suggests that if educators choose this as their justification for what they teach, then unless another reason can be given as to why this is an important aim in teaching, then teachers could be charged with imposing or indoctrinating a child into a particular way of life. White asks the question: 'Hasn't there been an arbitrary imposition on your part?' (1982, p. 41).

Indoctrination

The key word here of course is *arbitrary*, since a distinction is being made between indoctrination and education in terms of whether or not a justification can be provided for this particular form of the curriculum. A further assumption is made that the child is being inducted into some way of life – in other words, the child, as a learner, was in one state of being before undergoing the learning experience and in a different state of being after undergoing it – and that this does not constitute the distinguishing factor between indoctrination and education. It is the arbitrary nature of the imposition that constitutes the difference between the two. However, what I have suggested is that imposing a curriculum on a child which is focused on reflection and autonomy is not necessarily arbitrary because there are good reasons why this might contribute to achieving the good life, which by definition is sought by all.

If a distinction is to be maintained between indoctrination and education, where the latter is understood as involving some measure of autonomy, then an argument to justify this distinction has to be provided. Before I do this, a further objection should be noted. This is that an argument could be made for the indoctrination of the learner on the grounds that it is necessary if they are to exercise their autonomy after they have grown up and left school. Clearly, there is a sense in which both processes – learning how to be autonomous and being autonomous once one has learnt how – involve specific actions by the learner. Thus if autonomy is defined as the capacity to make sound judgements about the consequences of one's actions, then this doesn't just happen, but results from a series of actions on the part of the learner that are in some sense cumulative so that they are better able to make those sound judgements after the learning experiences than before. Thus the learner is provided with experiences, which if they successfully achieve their purpose, enable the learner to become autonomous, and they would not have become autonomous unless they had actually had those experiences. In short, for their own good as an educated person, and if it is justified that the optimum state of affairs for an adult is that they should exercise their autonomy, they should be indoctrinated into a way of life. There are many ifs and buts here in this argument and we need to address some of them.

It is not at all clear that a notion of education which involves the imposition of a particular state of mind on a child does in fact lead to the development of dispositions that in later life we might want to call autonomous. In part, this is an empirical matter, and yet even then we have to be sure that a causal relation that we have identified from an examination of what has in fact gone on in the past can allow us to predict what will happen in the future. We can make a judgement from knowledge of what has happened in the past that certain experiences do not in fact allow the individual to lead a full and autonomous life when they grow up because those experiences have in some sense damaged them. I am thinking here of child abuse in which the child has been so badly affected by his or her experiences as to be rendered unable to lead a fulfilled and happy life. That is the negative side of the matter. There is also the positive side, in which it is difficult to identify those experiences which might lead to the desired state of autonomy after the child has experienced them. It is tempting, however, to suggest that experiencing autonomy or being allowed to make those choices which constitute an autonomous life as a learner is a better way of learning to be autonomous than being told what to do.

The second area of difficulty revolves around the extent to which we can make sense of the idea of a non-indoctrinated child. Various attempts have been made to identify such a child and these have focused on the type of imposition afforded to the child. Hand (2002, p. 545) defines indoctrination in the following way: 'For to indoctrinate a child (in the sense in which I shall use this contested term) is precisely to impart beliefs to her in such a way that she holds them non-rationally, or without regard for evidence.'

We should note here that the definition focuses not on the justification for imposing such a state of mind but on the imparting of those beliefs to the child and it is the pedagogic relation which is the key to Hand's argument, and this is predicated on the way the child comes to hold those beliefs. So a child can have a religious faith as a result of having been inducted into that belief while at school, but they have been indoctrinated if they hold the belief without regard to the evidence. If put in this way, a problem with religious belief immediately occurs: it is hard to see what might constitute good reasons for such belief, and the belief, if this is accepted, would then be categorised as irrational, and would be consigned to the realm of indoctrination. Gardner (1988, p. 94) further refines the argument when he suggests that indoctrination comprises

> the production of a certain effect, and . . . this consists of a reluctance to change even in the face of arguments and reasons to which no response is forthcoming or in the face of arguments and evidence that, to an outsider, may seem overwhelming.

Two points should be noted here. The first of them is that an indoctrinated state of being is a psychological state in which the person is unable to change their mind or their belief system. The second is that the arguments and evidence for changing the person's mind constitute a public test where agreement is reached about what they are. There may be a less stringent test, which we can call the weaker argument, where the public test is forgone and replaced with a test involving the strength of the argument. If good reasons are provided as to why the person should change their mind, and this argument accepts that the capacity to change one's mind is a precondition of an autonomous state of being, then though the person may choose not to change their mind, they do so because the reasons that are provided do not constitute sufficient grounds for doing so. They are therefore still acting autonomously. This, however, still leaves us with a dilemma, which can be expressed in the form of a question: what might constitute a good reason for changing one's mind?

One possible answer is that we are committed to some form of coherence of argument about what we should do, and we might want to change our mind to produce a greater sense of coherence in our belief system. Another reason might be that our present state of being has led in the past to certain unhappy consequences, and we are seeking to develop a set of beliefs that in our judgement will produce happier consequences for us. A third set of reasons might focus on the notion that we are simply wrong in holding to the particular set of beliefs that we presently have and that we should therefore amend our beliefs so that they are more correct. A fourth set of reasons might focus on a desire to live our lives free from the dictates of reason; and we are thus committed to acting irrationally. In this last case, it should be noted that though we choose to act irrationally, all we are in fact doing is the mirror opposite of what the rational person might choose to do. Thus the criteria for determining what we do are in fact based on a system of rational thought and action, and we could not go on in life without accepting that there is a system of rationality. Finally, we might actually be confused about why we do this rather than that and thus the choices we make are essentially arbitrary. To equate autonomy with the making of choices is therefore problematic.

What is also problematic is to define the person acting in a non-autonomous way as someone not being open to rational persuasion. And this is because of the difficulty with identifying what a good reason for changing one's life or making choices might be. The argument made by faith philosophers is that it is possible to induct a child into a religious way of life without at the same time indoctrinating them. The counter-argument is that inducting a child into a religious faith is per se indoctrination because that person is now less open to changing their mind about their belief system, and the purpose of a liberal education is to open the mind to further possibilities rather than close it. Once again, we need to be aware that the person may still be acting autonomously even if they choose not to – they choose a life of slavery, to give one of White's examples. The problem with the dichotomous nature of the pair of words, indoctrination–education, is that any prescription about education involves the development of a set of presuppositions about how the child and the future adult should behave, and thus is essentially normative. It is to this argument that we now need to turn our attention.

Prescription

The reason we need to do this is because, if autonomy is to provide the underpinning rationale for what should constitute a curriculum, then first we need to be clear about what an autonomous life might be, and second, we need to be clear about why leading an autonomous life should be better than leading a non-autonomous life. If education, and certainly formal education, is defined as an intervention in the life of the child, then though that intervention may have unexpected and unplanned consequences, it is still designed to initiate the child into one form of life rather than another. This operates at the level of knowledge as well as at the level of skill or disposition. We cannot avoid the prescriptive nature of education, and this is because by choosing one set of skills or a particular knowledge agenda, we are necessarily putting to one side other knowledge or skill agendas. We might have good reasons for doing so, but the act of curriculum-making per se involves including some activities and excluding others.

We now come to the main thrust of the instrumentalist argument and this is that those experiences which should be incorporated into the curriculum can only be derived from a notion of what the good life is, in so far as the skills and knowledge needed to be acquired by children as they grow up are necessary for the living of the good life. Is it therefore possible to identify what that good life might be? We have already suggested that it is more than making choices or living the autonomous life, for two reasons. First, there may be moral or ethical reasons for sanctioning some forms of behaviour and supporting others. Second, in being autonomous individuals may make choices which do not lead to fulfilment in their lives. However, we have established the principle that however hard it is to define what the good life is, this end can be the only logical *raison d'être* for determining what is in the curriculum.

White wants to anchor this prescriptive activity in some notion of human nature. In effect there are three possible scenarios. The first of these is that human nature has a plasticity which does not allow us to say that human beings have dispositions which should be fulfilled. Human needs and wants are infinitely flexible and beyond the basics of survival, can be construed as irremediably social. They are in a sense therefore manufactured or at least the human need, want or desire comes about because of the way society is structured. The second scenario suggests the opposite, that the natural can be identified and this natural state of affairs persists and has persisted through time and place, and though we do not always know what we want, for example because we have misled ourselves or are confused about what we want, we can only understand these false beliefs in terms of a pure consciousness that seeks fulfilment. The third scenario is a variant on the second, in that there is an innate and natural sense of completeness built into human beings, which needs to be achieved if the good life is to be led, and though in most cases human beings do not achieve this, it does provide us with a measure to judge the state of affairs which we might want to call the good life. If we are to accept either or both of these last two scenarios, then further arguments or evidence would need to be provided to support such assertions.

The argument about education and the curriculum being based around a conception of the good life has taken the following form:

1   The good life is identified, though there may be a number of variants, and this means that it is not understood in the same way by everyone.

2   In order for a person, or a number of people, or the majority of people living together in a society to lead that good life to whatever degree, they need to have developed dispositions, skills and knowledge which enable them to make choices that allow them to lead the good life.

3   Further to this, society must be so arranged that individuals are able to make the appropriate choices, and, having made those choices, they can then lead the good life.

4   This is predicated on a further set of assumptions which is that the adult, when a child, was initiated through a series of appropriate experiences into a way of life which comprises having the right dispositions, developing the appropriate skills and acquiring the right type of knowledge.

5   Finally, this is further predicated on an assumption that people can retain those skills, dispositions and knowledge which they acquired during childhood into adulthood when they are actually leading the good life.

I have already suggested that many of these assumptions are problematic. For example, defining the good life is a major difficulty, since there are an almost infinite number of ways of doing this, corresponding to all the activities that human beings have in the past performed and all the activities that have not been invented yet that they might want to perform in the future. Incidentally, this problem is encapsulated in the observation that if a country adopts a national curriculum, every interest group in that country then provides an argument for including the activity that it is promoting in that curriculum. Choices therefore have to be made, and a rationale provided as to why some activities are included in the curriculum and others excluded.

A number of arguments can then be put forward as to what that good life should be, many of them quite weak in their persuasive force. If we simply want to assert that this is the life that we prefer, and that society should be so structured that our preferences are legitimated, then this is a clear case of special pleading, and comes up against the argument that it might prevent other people from leading the good life as they conceive it when their conception is different from our own. This argument could include the possibility of us making choices as a justification in its own right, in the sense that the good life consists of us making choices. The second argument is that we should make arrangements in society so that as many preferences can be adopted as is possible; logically, this means that society should be constructed so as to allow choices to be made. The reason why this follows from our basic premise is that if a number of different preferences are to be satisfied then they must be available and open to more than one person, and those people therefore must have the option of choosing between them. This second argument depends on two premises. The first is that people in society have different preferences (this is an empirical proposition) and thus could not be persuaded, cajoled or forced to develop the same set of preferences; and second, that their preference is an informed one, not in the sense that one way of life is better than another, but in the sense that they really do prefer one way of life over another, and are not going to change their mind a few days later. The third argument is that we should lead a particular way of life which is justified and rationalised either metaphysically, or because it is the natural way of doing things, or because it has some teleological purpose and thus our preferences, our special pleading, and our desire for choice should be put to one side to accommodate this.

It seems to me that each of these justifications has specific weaknesses. However, if we reframe the argument, then we can see that there is a possible way out of the dilemma. This reframing comprises an acceptance that we don't know what the good life consists of for any particular person until they are actually leading it, and furthermore we cannot say that one way of life is superior to another; however, what we can say is that formal education is a preparation for leading some form of life, whether good or bad, and therefore logically it must involve that person in being equipped to make choices, though this is no guarantee that those choices will lead to the good life being experienced. Post-modernism, in contrast, provides a different view of the curriculum.

Chapter 13

Post-modernism and the curriculum

> Animals are divided into: (a) belonging to the Emperor, (b) embalmed, (c) tame, (d) sucking pigs, (e) sirens, (f) fabulous, (g) stray dogs, (h) included in the present classification, (i) frenzied, (j) unnumerable, (k) drawn with a very fine camel hair brush, (l) et cetera, (m) having just broken the water pitcher, (n) that from a long way off look like flies.
>
> (Jorge-Luis Borges quoted in Foucault, 1977, p. xv)

This strange and disconcerting classificatory scheme can serve as an introduction to a different perspective on the curriculum from that provided by modernist thinkers such as W. J. Popham, Lawrence Stenhouse or Jerome Bruner. It has been hinted at by critical theorists such as Michael Apple and Henri Giroux, though never fully embraced by them, and it takes the debate about knowledge as an underpinning rationale for the curriculum down relativist and constructivist pathways. Though post-modernists thinkers come in a range of guises, post-modernism can be identified through a number of key underpinning principles.

For explanatory purposes, it is important to distinguish between a post-modern world and a post-modern way of knowing that world, in short between the ontology of the world and its epistemology, since the two are frequently conflated. A post-modern ontology suggests that fixed and stable values are no longer influential; that identities are decentred, that relations between individuals are unstable; that structures are emergent rather than relatively immune to change; and that progress in society is an illusion.

A post-modern epistemology or constructivist approach to the curriculum refers to how that reality can be known and therefore how this form of knowledge is reflected in the construction of a curriculum. Though post-modernist thinkers differ in their approaches, it is still possible to identify a range of views held in common by theorists who have described themselves as post-modernist or have been described as post-modernist by others. The first of these is a rejection of correspondence views of reality – the relationship between discourse and reality is fractured. Indeed, many leading post-modernist thinkers would subscribe to a view that Bhaskar (1979) calls radical relativism. Here, the only meaningful phenomenon is the text; and it cannot refer to an extra-discursive reality. The second of these principles is a distaste for universalising modes of thought and global narratives. Knowledge is local and specific, has no trans-social dimension to it, and is constructed within communities that develop their own criteria for determining what is true and what is false. Judgements made about other social settings and systems across place and time can only be made from the viewpoint of the social setting to which the observer belongs. Knowledge is therefore relative to particular time/space loci.

The third principle involves a rejection of ethical and teleological ideas. Foucault (1984, p. 9) suggests, for example, that

> [t]here is always something ludicrous in philosophical discourse when it tries, from the outside, to dictate for others, to tell them where their truth is and how to find it, or when it works up a case against them in the language of naïve positivity.

One of the consequences is that it then becomes impossible to identify progress in society, which may act as a driver for social change, but in reality merely replaces one social configuration with another. Given that post-modernists reject foundational principles, it is perhaps difficult to categorise a post-modern way of thinking, and this self-imposed lack of legitimacy is a serious problem. Frequently, post-modern ideas are criticised for claiming legitimacy and authority, as any set of ideas must do, and at the same time undermining that claim by denying credibility to these notions.

Adopting a post-modern perspective has certain implications; principally, that knowledge of the world cannot lead to the production of propositional, objective and verifiable knowledge that results in a science of pedagogy crossing physical, geographical and temporal boundaries. Doll (1989), for example, suggests that this view impacts on the curriculum in a number of ways: through open as opposed to closed systems; through the use of complex and cosmological concepts rather than simple, reductionist and separate conceptual schemata; and through notions of transformational rather than incremental change: 'an open system, on the other hand, needs fluxes, perturbations, anomalies, errors: these are the triggers which set off reorganisation' (Doll, 1989, p. 251).

Doll identifies four heuristic devices for characterising a post-modern rather then a modernist view of the curriculum. The first of these is that the curriculum should reflect new ways of understanding the world and move away from modernist, linear, functionalist means for both understanding the world and determining what it is. He puts it in the following way:

> I have argued that to break away from the modernist framework, in which the Tyler rationale is embedded, curricularists should, indeed must, study

contemporary developments in the fields of biology, chemistry, cognition, literary theory, mathematics and theology. In all these fields new models are emerging which pay attention to such issues as disequilibrium, internal structuration, pathways of development, and transformative reorganisation.

(Doll, 1989, p. 252)

These new models are ontologically distinct from modernist and Newtonian views of the world.

The second of Doll's heuristic devices suggests that because social development is punctuational and erratic, rather than linear and progressive, then pedagogy should in turn reflect this. Instead of lesson plans with beginnings, middles and endings, with pre-specified outcomes, and with determinate purposes, lessons should be explorative, avoid closure, create disequilibrium in the minds of students, and encourage multiple pathways and alternatives.

A third heuristic device would move beyond tidy behavioural objectives to structure lesson plans and the curriculum, and would be underpinned by broad general goals agreed and negotiated with all the parties involved, the community, parents, teachers and, more importantly, the students themselves. Finally, Doll suggests that the abiding concern of the pedagogic process should be interrelationships among persons, so that sharing and caring relationships become central to learning:

> Mutual inquiry, rather than the transmission of knowledge or production of specific behaviours, is the general framework in which this relationship would be placed. The process by which it is to grow and transform itself is that of dialectical interaction. In contrast to contingencies of reinforcement or mastery of predetermined techniques, dialectical interaction is, itself, the process in which learning takes place.
>
> (Doll, 1989, p. 252)

In short, he recommends weak insulations between teachers and those they teach and weak insulations between disciplinary knowledge and the knowledge that a person needs to go on in life.

Usher and Edwards (1997), in turn, identify five ways by which a post-modern curriculum could be constructed. Education should seek to be more diverse in relation to its goals and processes. As a consequence, a more flexible approach to its organisational structures, curricula and pedagogies should be adopted. Since unpredictability is the leitmotif of a post-modernist ontology, education cannot act to reproduce society or to control it, and the knowledge developed and produced in formal systems of education therefore should not reflect disciplinary knowledge structures. In support of this, they argue that: 'any attempt to place education into a straitjacket of uniform provision, standardised curricula, technicised teaching methods, and bearer of universal "messages" of rationality or modernity would be difficult to impose' (1997, p. 211).

Again, they suggest that participation in education should be diverse:

> Education in the postmodern, based as it is on cultural contexts, on localised and particular knowledges, on desires and on the valuing of experience of learning as an integral part of defining a 'lifestyle' cannot help but construct itself in a form which would better enable greater participation in a diversity of ways by culturally diverse learners.
>
> (1997, p. 212)

Finally, they argue for a general decentring and loosening of boundaries or at least a weakening of the forms of insulation established between subjects, teachers and learners. Both of these frameworks can act as powerful heuristics for designing a curriculum.

A post-modernist perspective seeks to subvert all foundations for knowledge, whether of a foundationalist or instrumental kind. It attempts to undermine and uncover those power–knowledge relations that underpin conventional research and curriculum construction. Lather's (1991) post-modern approach seeks to displace orthodoxy and in the process reconfigure curriculum knowledge in new ways. It attempts to: provide a space for alternative voices and undermine the priority usually given to the agendas held by powerful people in society; reveal the textual devices used in conventional curriculum texts and as a result attempt to show how powerful discourses are constructed; question how authors construct these texts and organise meanings, and again in the process show how language works to construct certain types of truths; challenge realist assumptions that there is a world 'out there' waiting to be discovered; explore the various possible ways of constructing alternative realities and identities; and be concerned with power and the politics of knowledge construction.

A post-modern approach would seek to deconstruct these linguistic and curricular forms – the use of binary oppositions which marginalise some forms of life at the expense of others; the attachment of evaluative connotations to particular words or phrases; the alignment of some ideas with others; the construction of boundaries round forms of thinking which act to exclude and marginalise – without at the same time putting in their place alternatives. Burbules (1995) suggests that the post-modern story may best be understood in relation to three narrative tropes: the ironic, the tragic and the parodic. The ironic trope is an attempt to indicate to the reader that meaning is never fixed or essentialised, and that the position he or she can take can never be definitive or natural. The tragic trope is an acknowledgement that any attempt to speak outside the comforting modernist assumptions enshrined in everyday and commonsense discourses is bound to be ambiguous, unsettling and incomplete. The third narrative trope identified by Burbules is the parodic where the only option open to individuals is to play the game without at any time taking up foundationalist or fixed positions about the curriculum. In effect, a post-modernist position is an extension of critical theory in so far as it acknowledges the concealed ideological position taken up by much modernist curriculum-making, but at the same time it refuses to accept that there are credible foundational alternatives.

This discursive frame is underpinned by a HyperTextual model of representation in which the introduction of new media, in particular the World Wide Web, is acting to reconfigure discursive arrangements and the place of the reader within them. Conventional models of textual production and consumption have privileged the writer over the reader. The World Wide Web has given us the possibility, though it is as yet hardly a revolution, of a more democratic relationship to the power of textual production which works on us and not through us. Landow (1992, pp. 70–1) coins the phrase 'this HyperTextual dissolution of centrality', and what he means by this is that new media allow the possibility of conversation rather than instruction so that no one ideology or agenda dominates any other: 'the figure of the HyperText author approaches, even if it does not entirely merge with, that of the reader; the functions of reader and writer become more deeply intertwined with each other than ever before.'

Landow (1992, p. 70) suggests that this comprises the merging of what has historically been two very different processes: 'Today when we consider reading and writing, we probably think of them as serial processes or as procedures carried out intermittently by the same person: first one reads, then one writes, and then one reads some more.' HyperText, which allows the possibility of having access to an almost infinite number of different texts produced by different authors, 'creates an active, even intrusive reader, carries this convergence of activities one step closer to completion; but in so doing, it infringes on the power of the writer, removing some of it and granting it to the reader'.

This ties HyperText more closely to what Rorty (1979, p. 70) has called an *edifying philosophy*, the point of which 'is to keep the conversation going rather than to find objective truth'. He goes on to suggest that this edifying philosophy makes sense

> only as a protest against attempts to close off conversation by proposals for universal commensuration through the hypostatization of some privileged set of descriptors. The danger which edifying discourse tries to avert is that some given vocabulary, some way in which people might come to think of themselves, will deceive them into thinking that from now on all discourse could be, or should be, normal discourse. The resulting freezing-over of culture would be, in the eyes of edifying philosophers, the dehumanization of human beings.

Rorty's passionate plea to abandon the quest for epistemological and therefore curriculum foundations still leaves the door open for new forms of curriculum knowledge and new ways of delivering it to be developed.

Studying the curriculum

These post-modernist frameworks suggest a series of questions for curriculum designers:

- What items of knowledge should be included in a curriculum and what items excluded?
- What reasons can be given for including some items of knowledge and excluding others?
- How should those items of knowledge be arranged in the curriculum?
- What is the relationship between items of knowledge within a curriculum and skills or dispositions that are taught as part of the curriculum?
- What is the relationship between disciplinary or academic knowledge and pedagogic knowledge?
- What types of arrangements in schools are suitable for delivery of the curriculum?
- What should be the strength of the insulations between different types of children, teachers and learners, teachers and educational managers, different types of knowledge, different items of domain-specific know-ledge, different types of skills, different educational purposes, different teaching episodes, different parts of the policy cycle and different organisational units?

It is the last of these questions which seems to me to be pivotal to an understanding of the curriculum. We need therefore to think through the implications of understanding the world of education in a Bernsteinian manner. By describing a curriculum in terms of the strength of the relation-ships between its different parts, there is a ready-made conceptual framework for analysing the different versions of the curriculum as they are enacted in different parts of the world. However, in the act of describing people, institutions, systems and curricula, and the relations between them, this necessarily involves the insertion of values into the process: description is never neutral, and this is because the process involves identifying and high-lighting some features of the person, institution, system or curriculum at the expense of others. Labelling, for example, acts as a way of establishing strong insulations between people, roles and functions, institutions and human relations. The designation of the object, and its attributes, is also going to have an effect on the types of relations that the object may enter into with other objects, and indeed the strength of those relations. Furthermore, in the act of describing something or someone, a process is started which gives the object the capacity to have powerful effects. Whether, of course, it exercises that power is a function of how its relations with other objects plays itself out over time. This is regardless of the objectivity of the dimension or category of the person or institution or idea, and indeed, as Bernstein suggests, the stronger the insulations between objects the more naturalised that property of the object becomes.

This implies a critical approach to the world and to curriculum-making; critical in the sense that any attempts at describing and explaining the world are fallible, and also because those ways of ordering the world, its categorisations and the relationships between them, cannot be justified in any absolute sense, and are always open to critique and their replacement by a different set of categories and relationships. Justin Cruickshank makes this point in the following way: '[c]ritical philosophy is therefore critical because it accepts neither the view that there are fixed philosophical first principles that guarantee epistemic certainty, nor the idea that first-order activities are self-justifying' (Cruickshank, 2002, p. 54). Cruickshank is arguing here for what he describes as an internal critique. Reality itself can never be known as such and thus any mirror image of the world is bound to fail. However, this picture theory of the world, with its designation of a correspondence relationship between the ontology of the world and its epistemology, can be replaced with a model of internal critique, so that, within existing frames of reference, current or even past ways of describing the world are shown to be flawed, and, therefore, potentially could be replaced by an infinite number of alternatives. However, each of these alternatives would in turn be subject to the internal critique, and cannot therefore provide epistemic certainty about the correctness of the ontological framework that is being proposed.

Curriculum ideologies

In this book, a number of different and at times conflicting curriculum ideologies have been identified: autonomous instrumentalism, critical instrumentalism, economic instrumentalism, disciplinary conventionalism, rational foundationalism, cultural foundationalism, psychological foundationalism and post-modernism. These are set out in Table 2, and compared in terms of a number of categories: pedagogic arrangements, relations between knowledge domains, knowledge or skill orientation, knowledge framing, progression and pacing, relations between teacher and taught, relations between types of learners, spatial and temporal arrangements, and criteria for evaluation.

Instrumentalism denotes a view of the curriculum that makes reference to a future state of affairs for the learner which is external to the setting in which the learning takes place. As we have noted in previous chapters, there are different types of instrumentalism and each variant is underpinned by a different set of principles. Thus, autonomous instrumentalism refers to a view of the curriculum in which the pedagogic arrangements, knowledge or skill

Table 2 Relations between curriculum rationales and pedagogic framing

	AI	CI	EI	DC	RF	CF	PF	PM
Pedagogic arrangements	Inquiry-based	Inquiry-based	Didactic	Didactic	Didactic	Didactic	Didactic	Inquiry-based
Relations between knowledge domains	Weak insulation	Weak insulation	Weak insulation	Strong insulation	Strong insulation	Strong insulation	Strong insulation	Weak insulation
Knowledge or skill/disposition orientation	Skill/disposition	Skill/disposition	Skill/disposition	Knowledge	Knowledge	Knowledge	Knowledge	Skill/disposition
Knowledge frame	Weak	Weak	Strong	Weak or strong	Strong	Strong	Strong	Weak
Progression and pacing	Weak	Weak	Strong	Strong	Strong	Strong	Strong	Weak
Relations between teacher and taught	Weak insulation	Weak insulation	Strong insulation	Either strong or weak insulation	Strong insulation	Strong insulation	Strong insulation	Weak insulation
Relations between types of learners	Weak insulation	Weak insulation	Strong insulation	Either strong or weak insulation	Weak insulation	Weak insulation	Weak insulation	Weak insulation
Spatial arrangements	Weakly marked	Weakly marked	Strongly marked	Strongly marked	Strongly marked	Strongly marked	Strongly marked	Weakly marked
Temporal arrangements	Weakly marked	Weakly marked	Strongly marked	Strongly marked	Strongly marked	Strongly marked	Strongly marked	Weakly marked
Criteria for evaluation	Implicit and unspecific	Implicit and unspecific	Explicit and specific	Either explicit or implicit	Explicit and specific	Explicit and specific	Explicit and specific	Implicit and unspecific

Note
Autonomous instrumentalism (AI); Critical instrumentalism (CI); Economic instrumentalism (EI); Disciplinary conventionalism (DC); Rational foundationalism (RF); Cultural foundationalism (CF); Psychological foundationalism (PF); Post-modernism (PM).

orientation, knowledge framing, relations between the knowledge domains, progression and pacing, relations between the teacher and the learner, relations between types of learners, spatial and temporal arrangements and the criteria for evaluation are determined by the principle that the end-product is an autonomous individual, or at least an individual who is able to exercise their autonomy, even if they choose not to or are prevented from doing so. Critical instrumentalism, in contrast, as a rationale for a curriculum and its internal relations, seeks to eliminate from society sources of inequality and unfairness. In other words, the purpose is directly political and learning is socially embedded. Economic instrumentalism above all prioritises the economic over other functions of society.

What I have sought to show in this book is that there is a variety of rationales for the curriculum, all of which have specific weaknesses. Conservative restorationists argue that the curriculum should be anchored in the past and they emphasise canons of influential texts, formal and didactic modes of pedagogy, the inculcation of values rooted in stability and hierarchy, strong insulations between disciplinary and everyday knowledge, strong forms of classification between different aspects of knowledge, and indeed in some cases a belief that curriculum knowledge is either intrinsically justified or even transcendental.

This points to what Young (2006) has described as the internalist fallacy, where it is argued that knowledge evolves only as an internal feature of the knowledge itself, so that conservative restorationists are able to 'defend existing orderings of knowledge and the social structures that they serve' (Young, 2006, p. 22). He contrasts this with what he describes as the externalist fallacy, or what I have called in this book instrumentalist approaches to the curriculum. The externalist fallacy treats all knowledge as provisional and contingent, and thus makes the mistake that curricular knowledge can only be identified in terms of specific social goals. These social goals may take a number of different forms, so critical theorists such as Michael Apple and Henri Giroux, as we have seen, can argue in the first place that the curriculum in the United States of America and in other parts of the world has been taken over by neo-conservatives holding sets of values with which they disagree, and in the second place, since all values are contingent, they should be replaced by a set of values which lead to a more socially just society. Young, as we have seen, subscribes neither to an internalist nor to an externalist position in his specification of what should be included in a curriculum, but believes that knowledge can be rooted in the ever-changing and evolving disciplines of knowledge and, in particular, in the transcendental conditions for knowledge production. Thus, he develops a set of curriculum desiderata:

1   The question of knowledge (what it is that people need to have the opportunity to learn in a school, college or university curriculum) must be central to any educational policy.

2   Knowledge about the world, if it is to be the basis of the curriculum involves concepts that take us beyond the contexts in which learners find themselves and those in which knowledge is acquired or produced.

3   The crucial implication of this idea of knowledge for the curriculum is that a distinction is essential between the theoretical knowledge produced by scientists and other specialists, usually within disciplines, and the everyday practical knowledge that people acquire through their experience in families, communities and workplaces. It is the former not the latter that must be at the heart of the curriculum. This, however, is not to denigrate the latter which is essential and superior to theoretical knowledge for everyday living in all societies.

4   The primary but not only purpose of educational institutions is to take people beyond their everyday knowledge and enable them to make sense of the world and their lives and explore alternatives; the purpose of educational institutions is not to celebrate, amplify or reproduce people's experience.

(Young, 2006, p. 22)

During the course of this book I have developed a number of arguments to suggest that Young's belief in the right conditions for the production of knowledge which both acts as a rationale for the curriculum and forms its content is mistaken. These were rehearsed in Chapter 5 above, and focus on Michel Foucault's arguments for an inextricable link between knowledge and power, despite the fact that he also suggests that knowledge has a universal basis. It is not just that knowledge is produced in circumstances which are undeniably social, but also that the criteria for distinguishing between true and false knowledge are socially located. For example, as Hacking (1999) so cogently argues, a statistical and chance view of the world only became possible with the development of disciplinary knowledge concerning the measurement of chance. If the right conditions for knowledge development cannot in the end provide a universalistic justification for the curriculum, then what we have left is instrumentalism.

The term *instrumentalism* has been used in this book to embrace a number of different positions and it is important to distinguish between the various forms. Economism refers to a justification for the curriculum which prioritises above all other ends of education the needs of the economy. Conservative restorationists seek to preserve a set of values rooted in the past. Humanist instrumentalists argue that the real justification for a curriculum rests on the development of a notion of autonomy, with the autonomous individual being the sine qua non of the ideal society. Critical theorists suggest that a curriculum has to be structured so that children develop identities congruent with the idea of social justice and this will result in the emergence of a more socially just society. All these different versions of instrumentalism, though rooted in different value-systems and educational purposes, are constructed through a particular type of argument. This argument has a number of stages: (a) a preferred vision of society is identified; (b) the conditions for the existence of such a society are then in turn identified; (c) the role of the education system and the contents and form that a curriculum should take to achieve these social ends are clarified; and (d) the means for the delivery of those ends having been identified are then enacted, resulting in changes to existing curricular forms and changes to society.

It is in relation to the third of these points that the contributions of Bernstein, Bruner and Vygotsky have been so influential. Bernstein's contention is that what constitutes curriculum and pedagogic knowledge is not so much its contents, but the relations between categories and in particular the strength of the insulation between them. It is this which determines the way pedagogic knowledge is delivered in schools, and thus forms the identities of learners in formal and informal educational settings. Bruner's frequent assertions that learning is an active, social and reciprocal activity has implications for the type of knowledge which forms the contents of a curriculum, the pedagogic means by which it is delivered and the way children in formal settings develop as human beings. Vygotsky's advocacy of a participation antithesis both suggests an optimum view of learning and has implications for the form that curriculum knowledge should take.

In contrast to these views, it is possible to suggest that governments round the world, though not exclusively so, have sought to reinforce strong boundaries between disciplinary and everyday knowledge in developing the contents of their curricula, and have reinforced strong insulations between learners, between learners and teachers, between knowledge domains and between institutions which focus on teaching and learning.

References

Adey, P. (1997) 'Dimensions of Progression in a Curriculum', *The Curriculum Journal*, 8, 3, pp. 367–92.

Alexander, J. (1995) *Fin de Siecle Social Theory: Relativism, Reduction and the Problem of Reason*, London and New York: Verso.

Apple, M. (1979) *Ideology and the Curriculum*, Boston Mass.: Routledge and Kegan Paul.

Apple, M. (1982) *Education and Power*, New York: Routledge.

Apple, M. (1988) *Teachers and Texts: A Political Economy of Class and Gender Relations in Education*, New York: Routledge.

Apple, M. (1995) 'Official Knowledge and the Growth of the Activist State', in P. Atkinson, B. Davies and S. Delamont (eds) *Discourse and Reproduction: Essays in Honour of Basil Bernstein*, Cresskill, NJ: Hampton Press.

Apple, M. (1996) *Cultural Politics and Education*, New York: Teachers College Press.

Apple, M. (2000) *Official Knowledge: Democratic Education in a Conservative Age*, New York: Routledge.

Archer, M. (1995) *Realist Social Theory: The Morphogenetic Approach*, Cambridge: Cambridge University Press.

Argyris, C. and Schon, D. (1978) *Theory in Practice: Increasing Professional Practice*, San Francisco, Calif.: Jossey-Bass.

Aristotle (1925) *Nicomachean Ethics (Ethica Nicomachea)*, trans. W. D. Ross, Oxford: Oxford University Press.

Ball, S. (2003) *Class Strategies and the Education Market: The Middle Classes and Social Advantage*, London: RoutledgeFalmer.

Bandura, A. (1986) *Social Foundations of Thought and Action*, Englewood Cliffs, NJ: Prentice-Hall.

Bernstein, B. (1971) 'On the Classification and Framing of Educational Knowledge', in M. Young (ed.) *Knowledge and Control: New Directions for the Sociology of Education*, London: Macmillan.

Bernstein, B. (1975) *Class, Codes and Control: Theoretical Studies Towards a Theory of Educational Transmission*, London: Routledge and Kegan Paul.

Bernstein, B. (1977) *Class, Codes and Control*, Volume 3, London: Routledge.

Bernstein, B. (1985) 'On Pedagogic Discourse', *Handbook of Theory and Research in the Sociology of Education*, New York: Greenwood Press.

Bernstein, B. (1990) *Class, Codes and Control: The Structuring of Pedagogic Discourse*, London: Routledge and Kegan Paul.

Bernstein, B. (1996) *Pedagogy, Symbolic Control and Identity: Theory, Research and Critique*, London: Taylor and Francis.

Bernstein, B. (2000) *Pedagogy, Symbolic Control and Identity: Theory, Research and Critique* (revised edition), London: Taylor and Francis.

Bhaskar, R. (1979) *The Possibility of Naturalism: A Philosophical Critique of the Contemporary Human Sciences*, London: Harvester.

Bhaskar, R. (1998) 'General Introduction', in M. Archer, R. Bhaskar, A. Collier, T. Lawson and A. Norris (eds) *Critical Realism: Essential Readings*, London: Routledge.

Bloom, B. and Krathwohl, D. (1956) *Taxonomy of Educational Objectives: The Classification of Educational Goals, by a Committee of College and University Examiners. Handbook I: Cognitive Domain*, London: Longmans, Green.

Bloom, B., Hastings, T. and Madaus, G. (1971) *Handbook of Summative and Formative Evaluation*, New York: McGraw Hill.

Bobbitt, F. (1913) 'Some General Principles of Management Applied to the Problems of City-school Systems', in *The Supervision of City Schools. Twelfth Yearbook of the National Society for the Study of Education*, Bloomington, Ill.: Public School Publishing Company.

Bobbitt, F. (1918) *The Curriculum*, Boston: Houghton Mifflin.

Bobbitt, F. (1924) *How to Make a Curriculum*, Boston: Houghton Mifflin.

Boud, D. and Walker, D. (1998) 'Making the Most of Experience', *Studies in Continuing Education*, 12, 2, pp. 61–80.

Bourdieu, P. and Passeron, J.-C. (1990) *Reproduction*, London: Sage.

Bowles, S. and Gintis, H. (eds) (1976) *Schooling in Capitalist America*, London: Routledge.

Bredo, E. (1999) 'Reconstructing Educational Psychology', in P. Murphy (ed.) *Learners, Learning and Assessment*, London: Sage Publications.

Brookfield, S. (1987) *Developing Critical Thinkers: Challenging Adults to Explore Alternative Ways of Thinking and Acting*, San Francisco, Calif.: Jossey-Bass.

Bruner, J. (1960) *The Process of Education*, Cambridge, Mass.: Harvard University Press.

Bruner, J. (1966) *Towards a Theory of Instruction*, Cambridge, Mass.: Harvard University Press.

Bruner, J. (1971) *The Relevance of Education*, New York: Norton.

Bruner, J. (1983) *In Search of Mind: Essays in Autobiography*, New York: Harper Row.

Bruner, J. (1996) *The Culture of Education*, Cambridge, Mass.: Harvard University Press.

Bucher, R. and Stelling, J. (1977) *Becoming Professional*, Beverly Hills, Calif.: Sage Publications.

Burbules, N. (1995) 'Postmodern Doubt and Philosophy of Education', unpublished paper, Philosophy of Education Society Annual Conference, San Francisco.

Callan, E. (1988) *Autonomy and Schooling*, Montreal: Kingston.

Carr, D. (1998) 'Introduction', in D. Carr (ed.) *Education, Knowledge and Truth: Beyond the Postmodern Impasse*, London: Routledge.

Charters, W. (1909) *Methods of Teaching: Developed from a Functional Standpoint*, Chicago: Row, Peterson.

Charters, W. (1923) *Curriculum Construction*, New York: Macmillan.

Chomsky, N. (1965) *Aspects of the Theory of Syntax*, Cambridge, Mass.: MIT Press.

Clayton, M. (1993) 'White on Autonomy, Neutrality and Well-Being', *Journal of Philosophy of Education*, 27, pp. 101–12.

Collins, A., Brown, J. S. and Newman, S. E. (1989) 'Cognitive Apprenticeship: Teaching the Crafts of Reading, Writing, and Mathematics', in L. B. Resnick (ed.) *Knowing, Learning, and Instruction: Essays in Honour of Robert Glaser*, Hillsdale, NJ: Lawrence Erlbaum Associates.

Creemers, B. (1994) 'The History, Value and Purpose of School Effectiveness Studies', in D. Reynolds, B. Creemers, P. Nesselradt, E. Shaffer, S. Stringfield and C. Teddlie (eds) *Advances in School Effectiveness: Research and Practice*, Oxford: Pergamon.

Cruickshank, J. (2002) 'Critical Realism and Critical Philosophy', *Journal of Critical Realism*, 1, 1, pp. 49–66.

Daniels, H. (2001) *Vygotsky and Pedagogy*, London: RoutledgeFalmer.

Diaz, M. (2001) 'Subject, Power and Pedagogic Discourse', in A. Morais, I. Neves, B. Davies and H. Daniels (eds) *Towards a Sociology of Pedagogy: The Contribution of Basil Bernstein to Research*, New York: Peter Lang.

Doll, W. E. (1989) 'Foundations for a Post-Modern Curriculum', *Journal of Curriculum Studies*, 21, 3, pp. 259–70.

Dunne, J. (1988) 'Teaching and Limits of Technique: An Analysis of the Behavioural Objectives Model', *The Irish Journal of Education*, 22, 2, pp. 66–90.

Elliott, J. (1998) *The Curriculum Experiment: Meeting the Challenge of Social Change*, Buckingham: Open University Press.

Fitz, J., Davies, B. and Evans, J. (2006) *Educational Policy and Social Reproduction*, London and New York: Routledge.

Flood, R. and Romm, N. (1996) *Diversity Management: Triple Loop Learning*, Chichester: Wiley.

Fogarty, R. (1991) *The Mindful School: How to Integrate the Curriculum*, Pallantine, Ill.: Skylight Publishing.

Foucault, M. (1970) *The Order of Things: An Archaeology of the Human Sciences*, New York: Vintage.

Foucault, M. (1977) *Discipline and Punish: The Birth of the Prison*, New York: Vintage.

Foucault, M. (1978) *The History of Sexuality*, Volume One: *An Introduction*, New York: Pantheon.

Foucault, M. (1984) 'Preface to the History of Sexuality, Volume Two', in P. Rabinow (ed.) *The Foucault Reader: An Introduction to Foucault's Thought*, London: Penguin.

Gadamer, H.-G. (1975) *Truth and Method*, London: Sheed and Ward.

Gagne, R. (1985) *The Conditions of Learning* (4th edn), New York: Holt, Rinehart and Winston.

Galton, M. and MacBeath, J. (2002) *A Life in Teaching: The Workloads of Primary Teachers*, Report for the National Union of Teachers, Cambridge: Faculty of Education, University of Cambridge.

Galton, M., Gray, J. and Rudduck, J. (2003) *Transfer and Transitions in the Middle Years of Schooling (7–14): Continuities and Discontinuities in Learning*, Research Report RR 443, Nottingham: Department for Education and Skills.

Gardner, H. (1983) *Frames of Mind*, New York: Basic Books.

Gardner, P. (1988) 'Religious Upbringing and the Liberal Ideal of Religious Autonomy', *Journal of Philosophy of Education*, 22, 1, pp. 83–98.

Giddens, A. (1984) *The Constitution of Society*, Cambridge: Polity Press.

Giroux, H. (1979) 'Schooling and the Culture of Positivism', *Educational Theory*, 29, 4, pp. 263–84.

Giroux, H. (1981) *Ideology, Culture and the Process of Teaching*, London: Falmer Press.

Giroux, H. (1983) *Theory and Resistance in Education*, London: Heinemann.

Giroux, H. (1988) *Teachers as Intellectuals: Toward a Critical Pedagogy of Learning*, Granby, Mass.: Bergin and Garvey.

Giroux, H. (1989) *Schooling for Democracy: Critical Pedagogy in the Modern Age*, London: Routledge.

Giroux, H. (1992) *Border Crossings: Cultural Workers and the Politics of Education*, London: Routledge.

Giroux, H. (1994) *Disturbing Pleasures: Learning Popular Culture*, London: Routledge.

Giroux, H. (1997) *Pedagogy and the Politics of Hope: Theory, Culture and Society*, Oxford and Border, Colo.: Westview Press.

Greene, M. (1973) *Teacher as Stranger*, Belmont, Calif.: Wadsworth.

Greene, M. (1978) *Landscapes of Learning*, New York: Teachers College Press.

Greene, M. (1988) *The Dialectic of Freedom*, New York: Teachers College Press.

Greene, M. (1995) *Releasing the Imagination: Essays on Education: The Arts and Social Change*, San Francisco, Calif.: Jossey-Bass.

Guile, D. and Young, M. (1999) 'Beyond the Institution of Apprenticeship: Towards a Social Theory of Learning as the Production of Knowledge', in P. Ainley and H. Rainbird (eds), *Apprenticeship. Towards a New Paradigm of Learning*, London: Kogan Page.

Habermas, J. (1987) *Knowledge and Human Interests*, Cambridge: Polity Press.

Hacking, I. (1981) 'Introduction', in I. Hacking (ed.) *Scientific Revolutions*, Oxford: Oxford University Press.

Hacking, I. (1999) *The Social Construction of What?*, Cambridge, Mass.: Harvard University Press.

Hand, M. (2002) 'Religious Upbringing Reconsidered', *Journal of Philosophy of Education*, 36, 4, pp. 545–57.

Hirst, P. (1969) 'The Logic of the Curriculum', *Journal of Curriculum Studies*, 1, 2, pp. 142–56.

Hirst, P. (1972) 'Liberal Education and Nature of Knowledge', in R. Dearden, P. Hirst and R. Peters (eds) *Education and Reason: Part Three of Education and the Development of Reason*, London and Boston: Routledge and Kegan Paul.

Hirst, P. (1974a) 'Educational Theory', in P. Hirst (ed.) *Educational Theory and its Foundation Disciplines*, London: Routledge and Kegan Paul.

Hirst, P. (1974b) *Knowledge and the Curriculum: A Collection of Philosophical Papers*, London: Routledge.

Hirst, P. (1993) 'Education, Knowledge and Practices', in R. Barrow and P. White (eds) *Beyond Liberal Education: Essays in Honour of Paul H. Hirst*, London: Routledge.

Kant, I. (1968) *The Critique of Pure Reason*, trans. N. Kemp Smith, London: Macmillan.

Kliebard, H. M. (1975) 'The Rise of Scientific Curriculum Making and its Aftermath', *Curriculum Theory Network*, 5, 1, pp. 27–38.

Kohlberg, L. (1976) 'Moral Stages and Moralization: The Cognitive-developmental

Approach', in T. Lickona (ed.) *Moral Development and Behaviour*, London: Holt, Rinehart and Winston.

Krathwohl, D., Bloom, B. and Masia, B. (1964) *Taxonomy of Educational Objectives: The Classification of Educational Goals. Handbook II: Affective Domain*, New York: David McKay.

Kysilka, M. (1998) 'Understanding Integrated Curriculum', *The Curriculum Journal*, 9, 2, pp. 197–210.

Landow, G. (1992) *The Convergence of Contemporary Critical Theory and Technology*, Baltimore, Md., and London: The Johns Hopkins University Press.

Langer, J. and Applebee, A. (1986) 'Reading and Writing Instruction: Toward a Theory of Teaching and Learning', in E. Z. Rothkopt (ed.) *Review of Research in Education*, 13, Washington, DC: American Educational Research Association.

Lankshear, C., Peters, M. and Knobel, M. (1996) 'Critical Pedagogy and Cyberspace', in H. Giroux, with C. Lankshear, P. McLaren and M. Peters (eds) *Counternarratives: Cultural Studies and Critical Pedagogies in Postmodern Spaces*, New York and London: Routledge.

Lather, P. (1991) *Feminist Research in Education*, Geelong: Deakin University Press.

Lave, J. and Wenger, E. (1991) *Situated Learning: Legitimate Peripheral Participation*, Cambridge: Cambridge University Press.

Lawton, D. (1989) *Education, Culture and the National Curriculum*, London: Hodder and Stoughton.

Lyotard, J.-F. (1984) *The Postmodern Condition: A Report on Knowledge*, Manchester: Manchester University Press.

MacIntyre, A. (1984) *After Virtue*, London: Gerald Duckworth.

MacIntyre, A. (1988) *Whose Justice? Which Rationality?*, London: Duckworth.

McLaren, P. (1989) *Life in Schools*, New York: Longman.

Matusov, E. (1998) 'When Solo Activity Is Not Privileged: Participation and Internalisation Models of Development', *Human Development*, 41, pp. 326–49.

Moll, L. C. (1990) 'Introduction', in L. C. Moll (ed.) *Vygotsky and Education: Instructional Implications and Applications of Sociohistorical Psychology*, Cambridge: Cambridge University Press.

Moore, A. (2000) *Teaching and Learning: Pedagogy, Curriculum and Culture*, London: RoutledgeFalmer.

Moore, R. (2005) *Education and Society: Issues and Explanations in the Sociology of Education*, Cambridge: Polity Press.

Moore, R. and Muller, J. (2002) 'The Growth of Knowledge and the Discursive Gap', *British Journal of Sociology of Education*, special edition: *Basil Bernstein's Theory of Class, Educational Codes and Social Control*, 23, 4, pp. 189–206.

Moore, R. and Young, M. F. D. (2001) 'Knowledge and the Curriculum in the Sociology of Education: Towards a Reconceptualisation', *British Journal of Sociology of Education*, 22, 4, pp. 445–61.

Nash, R. (2005) 'Explanation and Quantification in Educational Research: the Arguments of Critical and Scientific Realism', *British Educational Research Journal*, 31, 2, pp. 185–204.

Norwood Report (1943) *Curriculum and Examinations in Secondary Schools*, London: Her Majesty's Stationery Office.

Olssen, M. (2004) 'Doing Foucauldian Research in Education', in J. Marshall (ed.) *Poststructuralism, Philosophy and Pedagogy*, Dordrecht, Boston and London: Kluwer Academic Publishers.

Olssen, M., Codd, J. and O'Neill, A.-M. (2004) *Education Policy: Globalisation, Citizenship and Democracy*, London: Sage.

Palincsar, A. S. and Brown, A. L. (1988) 'Teaching and Practising Thinking Skills to Promote Comprehension in the Problem of Group Problem Solving', *Remedial and Special Education*, 9, 1, pp. 53–9.

Parkin, F. (1974) 'Strategies of Social Closure in Class Formation', in F. Parkin (ed.) *The Social Analysis of Class Structure*, London: Tavistock.

Parkin, F. (1979) *Marxism and Class Theory: A Bourgeois Critique*, London: Tavistock.

Piaget, J. (1971) *The Science of Education and the Psychology of the Child*, London: Routledge and Kegan Paul.

Popham, W. J. (1972) *An Evaluation Guidebook: A Set of Practical Guidelines for the Educational Evaluator*, Los Angeles: The Instructional Objectives Exchange.

Porpora, D. (1998) 'Four Concepts of Social Structure', in M. Archer, R. Bhaskar, A. Collier, T. Lawson and A. Norrie (eds) *Critical Realism: Essential Readings*, London and New York: Routledge.

Quine, W. (1953) *From a Logical Point of View*, New York: Harper and Row.

Rawls, J. (1971) *A Theory of Justice*, Oxford: Clarendon Press.

Rorty, R. (1979) *Philosophy and the Mirror of Nature*, Princeton, NJ: Princeton University Press.

Sammons, P., Thomas, S. and Mortimore, P. (1995) *Key Characteristics of Effectiveness: A Review of School Effectiveness Research*, London: Office of Standards in Education.

Sawicki, J. (1991) *Disciplining Foucault: Feminism, Power and the Body*, New York: Routledge.

Schon, D. (1983) *The Reflective Practitioner*, London: Temple Smith.

Schon, D. (1987) *Educating the Reflective Practitioner*, San Francisco, Calif.: Jossey-Bass.

Schon, D. (1992) 'The Theory of Enquiry: Dewey's Legacy to Education', *Curriculum Enquiry*, 22, 2, pp. 119–39.

Schwab, J. (1962) 'The Concept of the Structure of a Discipline', *Educational Record*, 43, pp. 197–205.

Schwab, J. (1969) 'The Practical: A Language for Curriculum', *School Review*, 79, pp. 493–542.

Schwab, J. (1971) 'The Practical: Arts of the Eclectic', *School Review*, 79, pp. 493–542.

Schwab, J. (1973) 'The Practical 3: Translation into Curriculum', *School Review*, 81, pp. 501–22.

Schwab, J. (1978) 'Education and the Structure of the Disciplines', in I. Westbury and N. Wilkof (eds) *Science, Curriculum and Liberal Education*, Chicago: University of Chicago Press.

Scott, D. (2000) 'Situated View of Learning' in C. Paechter, R. Edwards, R. Harrison and P. Twining (eds) *Learning, Space and Identity*, London: Paul Chapman Publishing.

Scott, D. (2003) 'Four Curriculum Discourses: A Genealogy of the Field', in D. Scott (ed.) *Curriculum Studies: Major Themes in Education*, London: RoutledgeFalmer.

Scott, D. (2005) 'Curriculum Models', in A. Moore (ed.) *Schooling, Society and Curriculum: New Directions for Curriculum Studies*, London: RoutledgeFalmer.

Scott, D., Lunt, I., Thorne, L. and Brown, A. (2004) *Professional Doctorates in Higher Education*, Buckingham: Open University Press.

Spens Report (1938) *Secondary Education: Grammar and Technical High Schools*, London: Her Majesty's Stationery Office.

Stenhouse, L. (1967) *Culture and Education*, London: Nelson Books.

Stenhouse, L. (1975) *An Introduction to Curriculum Research and Development*, London: Heinemann.

Strawson, P. (1959) *Individuals: An Essay in Descriptive Metaphysics*, London: Methuen.

Taylor, C. (1998) *Philosophy and the Human Sciences, Philosophical Papers 2*, Cambridge: Cambridge University Press.

Tharp, R. G. (1993) 'Institutional and Social Context of Educational Practice and Reform', in E. Forman, N. Minick and C. Stone (eds) *Contexts for Learning: Sociocultural Dynamics in Children's Development*, Oxford: Oxford University Press.

Tyler, R. (1950) *Basic Principles of Curriculum and Instruction*, Chicago: University of Chicago Press.

Tyler, R. (1968) *The Challenge of National Assessment*, Columbus, Ohio: Charles E. Merrill Publishing Company.

Usher, R. (1997) 'Telling a Story about Research and Research as Story-Telling: Postmodern Approaches to Social Research', in G. McKenzie, J. Powell and R. Usher (eds) *Understanding Social Research: Perspectives on Methodology and Practice*, London: Falmer Press.

Usher, R. and Edwards, R. (1997) *Postmodernism and Education*, London: Routledge.

Usher, R., Bryant, I. and Johnston, R. (1997) *Adult Education and the Post-modern Challenge: Learning beyond the Limits*, London: Routledge.

Vernon, P. (1957) *Secondary School Selection*, London: Methuen.

Vygotsky, L. (1978) *Mind in Society*, Cambridge, Mass.: Harvard University Press.

Vygotsky, L. (1987) *The Collected Works of L. S. Vygotsky, Volume 1: Problems of General Psychology*, ed. R. W. Rieber and A. Carton, New York: Plenum Press.

Vygotsky, L. (1991) *The Psychology of Art*, Cambridge, Mass.: The MIT Press.

Vygotsky, L. (1999) *Thought and Language*, Cambridge, Mass.: The MIT Press.

Webster, N. (1913) *Revised Unabridged Dictionary*, Springfield, Mass.: C. and G. Merriam.

Weiner, G. (1990) 'The Framing of School Knowledge: History in the National Curriculum', paper given at the British Educational Research Association Conference, Roehampton College, London, August.

Wenger, E. (1998) *Communities of Practice: Learning, Meaning, and Identity*, New York: Cambridge University Press.

White, J. (1973) *Towards a Compulsory Curriculum*, London: Routledge and Kegan Paul.

White, J. (1982) *The Aims of Education Revisited*, London: Routledge and Kegan Paul.

White, J. (1990) *Education and the Good Life: Beyond a National Curriculum*, London: Kogan Page.

White, J. (1997) *Education and the End of Work*, London: Cassell.

Whorf, B. (1954) *Language, Thought and Reality*, Boston, Mass.: MIT Press and New York: Wiley.

Winograd, T. and Flores, F. (1986) *Understanding Computers and Cognition*, Reading, Mass.: Addison-Wesley.

Wittgenstein, L. (1953) *Philosophical Investigations*, trans. G. E. M. Anscombe, Oxford: Blackwell.

Wittgenstein, L. (1961) *Tractatus Logico-Philosophicus*, trans. D. F. Pears and B. F. McGuinness, London: Routledge and Kegan Paul.

Wood, D. and Wood, H. (1996a) 'Commentary, Contingency in Tutoring and Learning', *Learning and Instruction*, 6, 4, pp. 391–7.

Wood, D. and Wood, H. (1996b) 'Vygotsky, Tutoring and Learning', *Oxford Review of Education*, 22, 1, pp. 5–16.

Wood, R. and Power, C. (1987) 'Aspects of the Competence-performance Distinction: Educational, Psychological and Measurement Issues', *Journal of Curriculum Studies*, 19, 5, pp. 409–24.

Yates, A. and Pidgeon, D. (1957) *Admission to Grammar School*, London: Newnes.

Young, M. F. D. (2006) 'Education, Knowledge and the Role of the State: The "Nationalisation" of Educational Knowledge', in A. Moore (ed.) *Schooling, Society and Curriculum*, London: RoutledgeFalmer.

Author index

Subject index

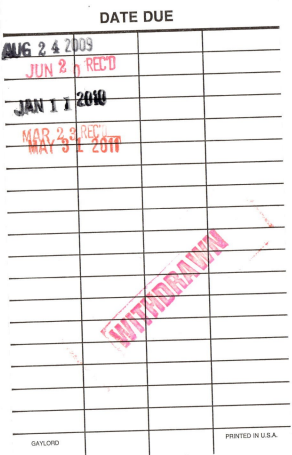